MW01283934

## Readers respond to T.

"Merlin Gonzales is a modern day Christian Renaissance man. He has taught multitudes of believers how to recognize a valid and relevant mission field right in their own communities. Our ministry has personally benefited from his expertise as a church consultant. In this book, *The Kingdom In Our Midst*, Merlin explores the realities of what the Kingdom of God looks like in our modern culture. He deals with various signs of the Kingdom, and the mandate to "take the land" for our Master and King, Jesus Christ. This book challenges the reader to operate in the supernatural realm of faith, and teaches principles of how to attract the favor of God and man. Reading and applying the information will prove to be life changing to any sincere seeker of the Kingdom."

—*BISHOP LEONARD SCOTT, Author, Soaring with Eagles,*
*Pastor Rock Community Church,*
*Founder and CEO Tyscot Music and Films*

"With encouraging stories, biblical truths, and practical applications, Merlin challenges us in his book to consider our legacy and to live out the Kingdom of God by being true missionaries to our own culture. There is such a need for this in our society and around the world, and Merlin's story of faith is a real example of what God can do with a person who is open to His will. Read it and be changed."

—*R. BOYD JOHNSON, PH.D., Chair, Graduate Studies in*
*Leadership, Indiana Wesleyan University*

"Merlin Gonzales understands the big picture about of how the Kingdom works with those in need. *The Kingdom In Our Midst* reignited my heart to be among the needy. He calls us to the simple and doable matter of being among those who are especially touched with God's Kingdom. I'm convinced your heart will be lit in the same way mine was as you read *The Kingdom in Our Midst*!"

—*STEVE SJOGREN, Author,*
*Conspiracy of Kindness, ServeCoach.com*

"I had the privilege of guiding Merlin in launching Faith Hope, and Love. Merlin has lived what he has written. His book and ministry is practical and prophetic. His example and written words point the big "C" Church smack into the center of God's will until Christ returns.

—*DANIEL BERNARD, Author, The Church at Its Best*
*President, Somebody Cares Tampa Bay*

"*The Kingdom In Our Midst*, like Merlin and Faith, Hope and Love, invokes the reader to live out their belief that Jesus is Lord. Like Jesus, we are called to open the table to all people, heal those in need of healing and praise Him. The book reminds us that the Master of the Universe is victorious because of love. He conquered his enemies not with force, but all are in awe of Him because of His love. We are called to love like Him, and the book reminds us of this and FHL is an outlet to live it!"

—*GABRIELLE NEAL, Program Director,*
*Catholic Charities Indianapolis*

"Merlin Gonzales exemplifies the Christian lifestyle by serving the needy, bringing unity to the Body of Christ and walking in miracles, signs and wonders. This book is a testimony of that lifestyle. Merlin shares his vision and strategies for changing a neighborhood, and challenges all of us to go on a mission right in our own backyard. If you want to impact your world, read this book."

—*LARRY & ELAINE LEONARD, Catch the Fire USA Mid-West Region Coordinators*


"In *The Kingdom In Our Midst*, Merlin Gonzales uses his own real-life experiences and the powerful insights he has gained to inspire the reader to embrace a simple but amazing expectation—that they, as well as every Christian, are equipped with the power of the Holy Spirit to make the Kingdom of God a truly tangible and visible presence in our world today!"

—*CHUCK EVANS, Pastor, the Church of Praise, Westfield, Indiana*

# The *Kingdom* In Our *Midst*

To John & Debbie

Luke 17:20-21

Merlin

# The Kingdom In Our Midst

## Living in God's Dominion
## Here on Earth

### Merlin Gonzales

faith hope Love

Connecting volunteers, resources and needs

Indianapolis, Indiana

The Kingdom In Our Midst
Merlin Gonzales

ISBN-13: 978-1480088085
ISBN-10: 1480088080

Library of Congress Control Number: 2012953977

Faith Hope and Love
8383 Craig Street, Suite 335
Indianapolis, IN 46250
317-578-3370
fhlinternational.org

Editor: Janet Schwind
Cover Design: Annie Gonzales, FOR HIS GLORY Designs
Interior Design: Suzanne Parada

## DEDICATION

I dedicate this book to Annie, my wife and best friend, whose faith keeps me strong. The joy in your life is contagious, inspiring anyone you come in contact with to pursue the source of it, our God All Mighty. You are beautiful.

To my children, Kayla and Andrew, who walk in integrity and honesty. Keep reaching for your passion and your desire to imitate our Savior, Jesus Christ.

To my parents, Cesar and Norma Gonzales, who have been examples of strength and perseverance. To my sisters, May Purnell and Maricar Duke, who have been there for our family.

And to the Holy Spirit who has guided me in writing this book and has been with me since I accepted Christ as my Savior.

# ACKNOWLEDGMENTS

I want to give thanks to the staff and leaders of Faith Hope and Love (FHL) who stood by me throughout the years and for believing in my calling to be a servant leader.

Thank you to the countless teachers, mentors and friends who have walked alongside me in my spiritual development... I think of Tim Beeson who has gone to the Lord; he was a catalyst to my spiritual breakthrough. My former pastor, Sean Tienhaara, who gave me confidence by acknowledging my calling. Skip Beyer, a spiritual friend and confidant, and Randy Gooder who has guided me in my church leadership higher education. Bob Irvin, who stood by me in the early years of FHL, whose contribution has sustained the ministry. Eldon Kibbey, my friend and advisor from the very start of our ministry. Elaine Leonard, for her invaluable input. Bill Lamb, a true servant of Christ whose heart for the lost ever beats with love and compassion. And, Donna Cherry who has been a good friend to my wife and I and has stood by us through good times and challenging times.

Special thanks to Janet Schwind for the great job in editing and for being my project manager for my first ever book. I would like to thank Suzanne Parada for a great interior book design and layout.

Thank you so much to my wife, Annie Gonzales, for her inspiring book cover design and for compiling the pictures in the book. You have captured the message of the book through your creative mind and heartfelt expression of art.

# CONTENTS

# PREFACE

My passion for the Kingdom of God to be tangible in our own lives propelled me to write this book. Although it is impossible for any human being to fully explain the Kingdom of God here on earth, we can see the glimpses of its invasion in our own backyards as we deepen our relationship with Him.

Every passing day of our lives is a day closer to the second coming of our Savior. This book is an attempt to usher His coming with great expectation. We are heaven's ambassadors and God's representatives on earth and so we actively participate in its expansion.

You and I are so privileged to co-labor in this mandate. The increasing presence of God is being experienced all over His creation through us by the power of the Holy Spirit. We will experience more of His presence as we dwell deeper in His love and as we walk in step with the Spirit. As we become more saturated with His character, His move will be our move and His desire will be our desire. He wants to ignite and empower those desires to be real in our lives. We are God's children, created in His image not only to inherit His Kingdom but also to expand the Kingdom in our midst.

**What IF?**

I have been curiously interviewing people about their idea of the Kingdom of God for many years. This notion of asking people their perspective began in the early 2000s. I began asking my home group members this question: "If you were given a chance of a lifetime, what would you do for your neighborhood?" More recently a friend told me that a pastor once asked, "What would your neighborhood look like if you could say, 'The Kingdom of God is here'?"

That question piqued my interest. I thought, *that's what I've wanted to ask all these years.* So I started asking people the question. I went all out. I started a contest online, spoke about it on TV and on radio, and interviewed people from all walks of life. This question brought me to city halls, churches, businesses, schools and people on the streets. I even had an opportunity to interview medical professionals in hospital rooms and patients in ICU. That same year, the Super Bowl was in Indianapolis and I had the opportunity to ask people from different parts of the United States. I have summarized some of the answers below.

What would your neighborhood look like if you could say,
"The Kingdom of God is here"?

Men's Bible group:

"A bunch of people worshipping and astonished before the Lord."

"Neighbors acknowledging each other."

" Getting to know each other and being able to serve by knowing what other people are going through."

"Desiring righteousness, peace and joy."

. . .

Indianapolis Mayor's Neighborhood Services:

"There would be a greater sense of peace and safety to take away the constant looking over your shoulder and constant concern for your family. Developing relationships with different parts of your community beyond just having religion and spirituality."

"You can better develop the sense of safety, which in turn fosters the moving of the Spirit. If we don't have relationship with God, it's hard to have relationship with others. But the opposite is true; if we don't have relationship with our neighbor, it's hard to have relationship with God. Oftentimes, the way that folks meet God is through their neighbors and through what they see in their neighbors' daily lives. You cannot meet God if you don't have relationship with somebody, even if it's the small business owner that sells gasoline at the corner; you could go through life and never see God. There would be very few needs, less crime and more love."

. . .

College students from Indianapolis universities:

"I envision our school as a place where everyone feels inspired to have a better education."

"Everyone could come to school feeling welcome and happy to be there."

"Having children feel the need to go to college and feel inspired and a sense of hope."

"You could walk outside at 3 a.m. not worrying that you may get shot or robbed."

"Everybody should be able to pursue their dream and attain them."

"God breathed life into the world so God is already present in the world. There would be more love and kindness, more philanthropy events, getting all our school work done and building a good future. Being able to meet the needs of classmates and the community as a whole."

. . .

A faith-based non-profit organization director:

"God's presence is active and alive in our neighborhoods and workplace. I feel we do have world peace. The world is not in turmoil. But where we can have peace is within ourselves and with our neighbors directly so each little corner of our world can have peace and that peace is God's love. We would have world peace because God's love is present. It would be a place of peace, joy, love and excitement. This community would be a refuge for the neglected and disadvantaged children, a place set apart to grow up healthy, loved, appreciated and a place where they come to know Jesus to change the future generation for Christ. Building a network of the Body of Christ to help build the campus for children."

. . .

A pastor's perspective:

"We would be a people of unity; there would be no difference based on race and any type of settings that would make one separate. People being treated equally; needs would go away because they will be taken care of by others or a neighbor next to you. There will be an end to what's wrong. More joy and peace, happiness. There would an end to destruction."

. . .

An executive of an international company:

"God is with us all the time. It's up to us to choose the right or wrong thing that will affect us. We need to help ourselves and others to make the right choices and it would be a growth spiral that makes community grow. The ability to see some of the athletes grow up from poverty or abuse and to help them to make good choices instead of resorting to violence in the streets. To encourage kids and give them the opportunity to see that there is a better life out there [South America] through our company-schools and having real life role models to change their lives."

. . .

From the 2012 Super Bowl Village:

"God is all around in many ways."

"There would be a lot less crime, no prejudice and less drama."

"God is already in my city; it's about your perspective. My church is multi-cultural and there is no discrimination."

"My city would look like heaven, loving each other and submitting to each other and to God."

. . .

In an ICU room in hospital:

The patient said, "There will be no judgment."

The medical professionals I interviewed said, "Laying hands on the sick and seeing them recover. I am sent with a Kingdom assignment here in my workplace. I don't just take care of patients; I know I am sent with a mission and a purpose. So I pray for patients and I see the Kingdom of God invading the hospitals with healings."

"The Kingdom of God would manifest through the actions of God's people. Miracles still happen in hospitals; along with miracles, God has gifted His people with knowledge and the ability to treat sickness and disease so it goes hand in hand. It is equally miraculous that God has gifted His people to do amazing things medically as well. I believe that's God reaching out in miraculous ways."

. . .

In a restaurant, a waitress's perspective:

"People would be more real and less fake. Believing in religion and not just putting on a show for everybody. This should be a happier place and real good food!"

. . .

From mayors in Central Indiana:

"I think the presence of God is already here in my city. However, if every one of us is more aware of the presence of God and would act more Christ-like, we would have a much better neighborhood. We would treat each other better, we would not prejudge people. Treat others like you want to be treated."

"If all of us are conscious of God's presence it definitely would be a better community. People will be more courteous with each other and be able to enjoy God's nature. Better neighborhood, serving people."

"Surely, the Lord is in this place."

———

It was an amazing period of time to hear the perspectives of different people about the Kingdom of God. One answer that stood out was when one of the mayors said that his city would be a better place if everyone would be aware, be conscious of God's presence and be Christ-like. A few days after my interview with him, it seemed the Lord had guided me to read Genesis 28, when Isaac sent Jacob to his Uncle Laban back in Paddan-Aram. Jacob's reasons were to run away from his brother Esau whom he had tricked into selling his birthright and stole his blessing, and to look for a wife there. On the way there, Jacob stopped at sundown at a place called Luz, which later became Bethel. He fell asleep and had a dream where he saw a stairway that reached to heaven. He saw angels going up and down the stairway. At the top of the ladder, he saw the Lord, who spoke to him. God said that that place belonged to him [Jacob] and that his descendants would be so many, it would be impossible to count them.

Then verse 16: When Jacob awoke from his sleep, he thought, "Surely the LORD is in this place, and I was not aware of it."

Could it be that the Kingdom of God is everywhere and we are just not aware of it or we refuse to wake up to it? I wonder if many of us have not woken up and realized that God is already present in our neighborhoods.

Volunteer Janet Schwind with Katrina refugee.

What would our cities look like if there was more awareness of God rather than the evil in the world? How would people interact with each other? What activities would dominate our country? What kind of impact would our churches have if all the Christians became the conduit of God's awareness wherever they go? What kind of political policies would our city halls have if the top politicians became cognizant of the Kingdom of God? What would the entertainment world look like? What kinds of songs would they sing, what kinds of sports would be popular and how would movies be made? What kinds of news would dominate the front page of a newspaper? Would we still see negative and horrible stories but see them compelling people to do good? Or perhaps the nature of the news would change—inspiring and positive stories that would encourage more people to be participants in advancing the Kingdom of God.

It would be interesting to see how the Internet and social media would function to serve the world. What would be the next types of business to thrive? Would there be more miracles, healings, signs and wonders? Could we actually say that more of heaven on earth is tangible in our communities? Or would it be just another nice Christian phrase? Would there be more churches, hospitals or prisons? I wonder what our crops and harvests would look like. Would the fruits be sweeter and would a bunch of grapes be so big that two men would have to hoist it on a pole to carry it (Numbers 13:23)?

Would our children be healthier, more vibrant, energetic and apt to live with Kingdom perspectives? Would our parents have peace of mind knowing their children are safe in school? Would our schools and universities teach more about creation instead of evolution? Would there be more prayers in educational institutions at the start and end of each day? Would the next generation advance the culture of heaven more than the world's norm? What would be their worldview? What would our country look like 10 or 20 years from now? If more people were aware of His presence, would our world be better or worse then? Would there be more pain and suffering or more joy and abundance?

Volunteers serving at neighborhood cleanup.

Volunteer Ethan Crane praying for homeless.

Let's explore the possibilities together. In this book, we will read stories of actual events that happened in the past few years. We will look at several Bible verses, quotes and references in anticipation of what our neighborhoods would look like if the Kingdom was in our midst. Let's venture together.

# PART ONE

What does the

Kingdom of God

look like?

The coming of the kingdom of God is not something that can be observed,
nor will people say, 'Here it is,' or 'There it is,' because the kingdom
of God is in your midst.

–LUKE 17:20-21

Recently I spoke with a friend of mine who pastors a church in Indianapolis. He used to belong to a group of pastors in the area who meet regularly for support and to pray for each other. He mentioned to me that the term "Kingdom of God" has been so overused in the clergy world that when someone starts to talk about it, some people actually lose interest in the conversation. How sad, I thought. How could a phrase that is so powerful become a byword to people in the church? Did the conversation become a theological battlefield with endless hours of reasoning and debate? Were their theologies and denominations getting in the way of pursuing the Kingdom? Is the topic so humongous that it simply becomes more confusing in our conversations? Is it because it remains only a subject of discussion but lacks evidence of its application and therefore continues to be removed far from reality? These questions kept haunting my mind over the past few years.

## The setup

During my first two years as a Christian, I started to challenge myself to apply what I had been learning from sermons, personal studies and Bible study group. One time I asked our Bible study group, "When do we get to do this stuff?" I began asking the Lord to give me opportunities to actually see the Kingdom in action. I wanted to test what I learned and to prove to myself that this thing really works. I had been asking myself, why is it that I only hear and read about spiritual people and authors who had God encounters but I have not had any personal experience? Were these miracles and God-encounter moments reserved only for those who are mature spiritually and had formal training? Or are they available to those who are hungry for the tangible manifestation of the Kingdom?

I was always fascinated by the supernatural and miracles since I was a little boy growing up in the Philippines. I wanted more than just learning but to actually experience those things in my life. My quest to find the answers to my questions would soon come.

Not long after my request to God, my wife Annie had a procedure in a hospital. I brought my Bible to catch up on my reading assignment. I sat in a waiting room full of people and started reading. I was just beginning to understand a few verses in the Bible when I felt a tap on my shoulder. I looked up and saw this young college student wearing a white scrub saying that I could now visit my wife in a recovery room. It was a simple procedure and it did not take the doctor long to do what needed to be done. On the way to the recovery room, I told the young man that he would be making good money in the near future. "Why?" he asked.

"Because you are studying to be a doctor," I answered.

He chuckled and told me that he is not studying to be a doctor. "I am just volunteering here," he said.

Somehow, that sentence intrigued me. As we continued our way to the recovery room, I asked him, "How do you feel volunteering and not getting paid in a place where people are making lots of money, especially the doctors and many other medical professionals?"

His answer got me thinking even more: "I receive more than what money can buy." I thought, *This boy is crazy!*

My mind started producing more questions... Why would a young person like him volunteer? He could be out there doing what other college students do—studying, partying and just enjoying life rather than working without getting paid. *There must be some Truth to his answer*, I thought to myself.

Before we arrived at the recovery room, I got all the information I needed from him. But I was determined to find out more about this "volunteerism thing."

The procedure was successful and my wife needed more time to recuperate in the room before we headed home. I spent a few minutes beside her, but my curiosity kept at me. I decided to visit the volunteer office.

The room was quiet with a few chairs and a couple of long tables. The volunteer coordinator came out to greet me, and I mentioned to her that I wanted to find out more about volunteering in the hospital. She talked a little bit and before I knew it, she handed me a form to fill out! Hesitantly, I filled it out and gave it back to her. After reviewing my application, she suggested that I could visit almost any patients in the hospital! I asked her why she thought of me visiting patients. She smiled and said it was because I was holding a Bible. "Can I also pray for them?" I asked. She said yes and I thought, *This is great—I can pray for the patients and put my learning into action!* She gave me a couple more papers to fill out and some medical forms to take to the lab for my physical and medical check-up. Within two weeks, I started to volunteer and was visiting patients for three hours a week. God had set me up!

## "A miracle"

Since that first Sunday I volunteered, I never looked back. It became my habit to stop by the hospital chapel before visiting any patients. I would typically ask God to lead me to the right persons and to give me the right words of encouragement for them. I enjoyed visiting people and prayed for them whenever they allowed me to. I brought my Bible everywhere in the hospital but seldom used it because I became so involved in conversations that I forgot to read verses with them; I just shared with them some verses that came to mind. However, I never backed down from asking every patient if I could pray for him or her. Most of them agreed to be prayed for.

I really enjoyed having conversations with patients and, sometimes, their families and friends. It was also interesting for me to find out about sicknesses, how the people were being treated and how they were coping with it. Sometimes it was sad to see patients who didn't have any family or friends in town to visit them. I would normally stay longer with them and keep them company. Most of the patients were very appreciative of being visited and prayed for.

After three short months, I had seen many patients with different kinds of health issues. I developed some close friendships with a few of them. It helped me to set my perspective in the right direction. Life is fragile and life is short. You never know when your time here on earth will end. I've heard stories of patients who were healthy and in an instant became paralyzed by a disease or an accident. I became friends with a few nurses and they came to know me as "the man who prays for people."

One fall afternoon, I stopped by the hospital chapel, as it had been my routine before visiting patients. As usual, I prayed that God would guide my steps to the right people and that He would teach me His ways. Three hours went by fast, visiting and praying for patients. I just had a few minutes to exchange pleasantries with some nurses and had decided to go home. While I was in the elevator, I somehow audibly heard to go back.

As I stepped out of the elevator at the ground floor, the urge got stronger to go back. But where will I go?

I got back in the elevator asking the Lord where He wanted me to go. This conversation with Him seldom happened to me. As I was asking Him where I should go, the elevator suddenly opened at the top floor. I stepped out and said "hi" to a nurse at the nurses' station. I did not know where to go so I went to a room where an out-of-town patient stays. I had visited her for several weeks and had watched her body deteriorate fast. *She must be the reason why I came back up*, I thought to myself.

We spoke for a few minutes when suddenly I heard loud banging from down the hall. I heard the voice of a woman shouting "Why?" over and over again. After a minute or two, I heard footsteps coming toward the room where I was. Suddenly, I felt I would be called to go to the room where there was a lot of commotion and medical people going in and out. I thought to myself, *I am not ready for this*.

Immediately after I had my silent conversation with the Lord, a nurse came rushing into the room. "I know you are not clergy but I know you pray for people. I need you to pray for the patient two rooms down!" I did not even have time to respond to her and I followed her immediately. As we were walking down the hallway, I had a quick conversation with God. I told Him I wasn't ready for this and I didn't know what to do. In fact, I didn't even know what was happening in that room. My conversation with him was interrupted when I peeked in through the doorway of this particular room—it felt cold, eerie, and it was chaotic! In the room were nurses, doctors and other medical professionals frantically trying to resuscitate a man. Some were going in and out of the room and some were attending to the patient. There were all kinds of medical machines, an oxygen tank and masks being moved around. I saw the mother of the patient pounding her hand on the wall screaming "Why?" and other words I could not understand. My frazzled mind quickly argued with God that I would not go in there and be in the way of medical professionals—I would not interrupt what they were doing to bring this man back to life!

The scene before me was utterly shocking. I looked at the patient. He was in his late 20s or early 30s. He was lying face up, positioned with his head at the foot end of the bed, fully naked and blue in the face. His mouth was foaming with white, thick saliva. His stiff body shook violently. Somehow, I focused my attention on his eyes, which were rolled back into his head, showing only the white part. Though he could not focus, his eyes somehow were piercing my soul while staring at me. In a split second, I knew he could not see me but it seemed like his eyes were sending signals to me. They were conflicting messages! One message was begging me to help him while the other told me to go away and leave him alone. It was a bizarre moment for me and I did not know what to make of it.

Suddenly, I saw a path cleared for me to walk toward him. The room suddenly got quiet and it seemed like everyone froze as I approached him. It was like a moment in time when someone hit a "pause" button. I placed my hand on his head as I was kneeling down. I prayed quietly, "God, heal this man" and quickly got up to get out of the way of everyone. Simultaneously as I was getting up, the room got busy and loud again. Then, as I took my first step away from the patient, the room suddenly got quiet again. You could hear a pin drop in the room! I saw everyone was looking at the patient. No one was talking or moving; his mother stopped shouting and banging on the wall. I looked back to see what had happened. To my amazement, the man stopped shaking and stopped foaming at the mouth. In an instant, his color had returned to normal and his body was relaxed. I could not believe my eyes witnessing all of this. I went back outside the room while wondering what had just happened.

I don't remember much of what transpired afterward. I went to visit another patient as my mind was trying to process that intense moment. After the medical professionals left, I walked back to the room of the "emergency" patient who was now in his calm condition. He seemed like he was a different man. His mother was next to him rubbing his head gently while looking at me. He said "Thank you" in the most heartfelt way. His mother thanked me also. After a few minutes, I left the room and was still in a state of astonishment. One of the things that puzzled me was that he knew me! He could not have seen me with his eyes rolled back when I prayed for him; they were all white! And because of his condition during that chaotic time he could not have seen me at all!

### "It couldn't be me"

On my way home, I called my wife and told her what just happened at the hospital. She was excited to hear about it. She said, "The Lord is using you!"

"It couldn't be me!" I replied. "It was a coincidence... I was just there at the right time." Then she asked me to repeat the entire story again to her, which I did, and she said that it was not a coincidence. Yet I still didn't believe that God was using me. So my wife asked me a third time to tell the entire story again. She said that the sequence of events was divinely scheduled and designed so that those present would encounter the power of

God in the room. I was sent there for an assignment. She said even though I felt I was not ready, I was obedient to do as He had asked me to do. I started to believe that this little ole me was now being used by God! I saw the Kingdom of God in action that night!

My faith got stronger after that weekend. Over the next few months, it seemed like I prayed for more people than I ever did in my entire life. Since then, I have seen many miracles in that hospital. Not everyone that I prayed for got healed but I've seen the power of God invade the heart of every patient I prayed for. Just what *is* the Kingdom of God? We will explore this topic next.

God will set up circumstances in our lives and will answer our prayers. Our part is to seek His heart and to respond to Him.

———

## The dominion of God

I had read about and studied the Kingdom of God during my church leadership education over the past few years. I thank God for the godly men and women who were Spirit-inspired to write reference materials, textbooks and well-researched publications. Thanks to the Christian universities and churches that continue to advance the building of a solid biblical foundation in our society.

Scholars have agreed that the Kingdom of God is the major focus of Jesus' teaching. It is so infinitely broad that we will be able to cover just a speck of it. Jesus ushered in the Kingdom during His first coming to earth, saying, *"The time is fulfilled, and the kingdom of God is at hand. Repent, and believe in the gospel"* (Mark 1:15, NKJV).

The term "kingdom" has been used since the very beginning of Israelite history. The Jews also learned from the Old Testament that the Messiah, or the Savior, would come. They knew that God was their king and He reigns on earth: *Say among the nations, "The LORD reigns"* (Psalm 96:10a). They were reminded of this scripture when Jesus proclaimed the inauguration of the Kingdom of God on earth.

During the time of Jesus, Israel had been waiting for a king to topple the rule of the Romans. Since the split of the Israelite empire after King David, the Israelites had gone through many kingdom takeovers, assassinations, ambushes, and head-on battles. They experienced defeats and victories. Many kings had oppressed them. They experienced captivity for 70 years outside of their own country. They had been controlled and denied their complete freedom. However, they knew that God had promised them a victorious kingdom. They had been anticipating a king who would fulfill the scripture to release them from their captivity and that they would see the *"day of God's anger against their enemies"* (Isaiah 61:2b, NLT).

Because of their past experience, they developed the idea of having a king rescue them to their freedom so they could establish their own religious and political agenda, to enjoy a better life and that they "be the head and not the tail." They looked to the day when they would have influence in the governance of the land and would share the authority of their country. They were looking forward to a kingdom based on their standards, tradition and values. Instead of the foreign rulers, they would be in control of their policy-making, rules and regulations and their destiny. It would be a kingdom based on their terms, their reasoning and their way of life.

From their perspective, it was rightly so to think that way. Many foreign kings had dominated them in the past and their time to rise up was coming. They felt that during Jesus' time, the time was ripe to overthrow the Romans. The time had now come to rise up and take control of their fate. Their king would soon come!

## A Kingdom not of this world

When Jesus spoke of the Kingdom, however, the Pharisees and the teachers of the law were perplexed because He spoke of a different kind of kingdom than what they had been expecting—one ruled by a human king. What Jesus announced was a Kingdom established and ruled by God, different than a world ruled by man. Through the Parables, He revealed that the Kingdom would be "God's way of doing things."

Jesus introduced a kingdom different than the world's standard. His Kingdom would be based on how He rules and reigns. It would be based on His character, values and standards. Love instead of hate would spread throughout the land. It would be a Kingdom that engages everyone to care for each other, to feed the hungry, to clothe the naked and to take care of the orphans, the widows, the aliens and the disadvantaged. Their neighborhoods would be cleaner, places where joy abounds, where they would not exploit nature, and they would find ways to preserve creation instead of destroying it. Material things would be secondary to their relationship with their king and with each other. There would be more giving than receiving, forgiveness rather than revenge, and kindness over hate. The Kingdom that Jesus proclaimed would not tolerate injustice, pride, abuse, nor any kind of evil.

Jesus provided teachings on how to live our lives and how to apply His principles in practical ways any time, wherever we are. His Sermon on the Mount taught us true righteousness that begins internally in the heart, not an external way of following rules and regulations. That's why Jesus said, *"You are like whitewashed tombs, which look beautiful on the outside but on the inside are full of the bones of the dead and everything unclean"* (Matthew 23:27b). The Kingdom that He was announcing is counter-culture, opposite from the teachers of the law, the Pharisees and the Sadducees' worldview. It would be a Kingdom ruled by God and not by men!

### New way of doing ministry

The Kingdom of God comes in countless ways. A few years ago, our ministry Faith Hope and Love (FHL) partnered with a church to have a neighborhood food pantry. We wrote some guidelines and procedures. We inventoried the food items and prepared forms to be filled out by the clients. We made sure the food pantry site was cleaned and organized before the starting time. Everyone was rushing to make sure that the food pantry leader who was from the church was satisfied. By the time we opened, the atmosphere of the environment was tense. However, when the clients started to come in, the place looked wonderful. Food was methodically arranged, grocery bags were prepared, registration forms were numbered and volunteers were ready.

We were able to serve all the clients by the end of the day. During the entire event though, people were uneasy and no meaningful relationships were established. Externally, the food pantry ran smoothly, but internally it was empty. The clients got their food and left right away.

Over the following year we learned that people, no matter how poor they are, value relationship more than the food. They want to be recognized and be noticed. They need food but they crave the relationships with others. They want to be welcomed and to be a part of something bigger than themselves. I found out that most of them don't just want to receive food. They want to have conversations with the volunteers. They don't want to be preached at but are more open to be prayed for and many of them wanted to help out when asked.

For many months, we continued our food pantries in partnership with different churches and organizations to feed the hungry. Since we did not have a physical office and location yet, we worked hard every time to gather and deliver grocery items to our partners' locations. The average number of families we served monthly was more than 100. With just two or three volunteers available to help in the initial setup, we worked 12-15 hours during the day of the pantry.

Within two years of on-the-job training, God showed me better ways to do food pantries. There are things that you need to go through yourself before you can be promoted to the next level. This was one of them for me. I thought, why not partner with organizations to establish self-sustained food pantries in the city? In this way, we can serve more people and be able to multiply the number of volunteers. Through them, we can also partner with local communities to gather more resources. Plus, we won't have to work as hard but we will be able to feed more people.

So, I decided to provide the groceries, manpower and training to our partners but with an agreement that within 6-9 months, our partner should be self- sustained. This means that they should have their own suppliers of pantry items, partners and donors, volunteer base, and be able to sustain the relationships with their own neighborhoods on an ongoing basis. Our ministry would help them connect with the local community to receive food and recruit volunteers. This food pantry would be operated by and for the community.

By the time of this writing, we have been instrumental in starting and establishing three self-sustained food pantries in Indianapolis. We are looking to plant several more this year. In the last Section of this book, I will explain why I feel the need to plant more food pantries in our cities.

## A radical way of living

Though Jesus might have been able to speak two or three languages, it is very likely that most of his teaching was given in Aramaic, for that was the language that most people in Palestine knew best. The gospels were written in Greek, of course, like the rest of the New Testament, and we therefore have no direct record of the actual Aramaic words used by Jesus. But even the Greek word that is translated into English as "kingdom"— *basileia*—often means more the *activity* of a king rather than the territory over which a sovereign might rule. The Aramaic word that most scholars think Jesus himself would have used— *malkutha*—certainly had that meaning:[1]

---

1    See John Drane, *Introducing the New Testament*, 113

Several times the RSV renders *basileia* by the English word "kingship" or "kingly power" (Lk 19-12; 23-42; Jn 18:36; Rev 17:12). The meaning "reign" or "rule" is obvious in other passages.[2] The coming of the Kingdom for which we pray in the Lord's Prayer means that God's will be done on earth, i.e., that his rule be perfectly realized (Mt 6:10). This is important for the interpretation of Jesus' message, for one of the major problems is that of how the Kingdom of God can be both future and present. If the Kingdom is primarily the *eschaton*—the "end of time" era of salvation—it is difficult to see how this future realm can also be present. However, we have seen that both in the Old Testament and in rabbinic Judaism, God's Kingdom— his reign—can have more than one meaning. God is now the King, but he must also *become* King.[3] Eschaton came from the Greek word *eskhaton*, which means "divinely ordained climax of history," or, end of the world, end of time, climax of history (dictionary.com).

"The coming of the kingdom of God is not something that can be observed, nor will people say, 'Here it is,' or 'There it is,' because the kingdom of God is in your midst"

This idea also supports what Jesus said in Luke 17:20-21: Once, on being asked by the Pharisees when the kingdom of God would come, Jesus replied, *"The coming of the kingdom of God is not something that can be observed, nor will people say,*

---

2    See G.E. Ladd, *Jesus and the Kingdom*, 130.
3    See G.E. Ladd, *A Theology of the New Testament*, 61

*'Here it is,' or 'There it is,' because the kingdom of God is in your midst"*. The other translations of the end of verse 21 are, *"For the Kingdom of God is already among you"*(NLT), and *"For indeed, the kingdom of God is within you"* (NKJV).

These verses challenged the Pharisees and the teachers of the Law. How could a kingdom be within a person or in their midst? They had been observing and anticipating the coming of this kingdom and yet Jesus said it *"is not something that can be observed."*

Take for example Nicodemus, a Jewish religious leader who observed Jesus and His works. Not all the Pharisees were hypocrites as one may speculate from Jesus' comments in various parts of the New Testament. Nicodemus, a Pharisee who was looking for information, experienced transformation when he encountered Jesus one evening (John 3:1-21). Later in the Gospel of John, Nicodemus spoke up about Jesus' innocence (John 7:45-53) and he helped Joseph of Arimathea retrieve the body of Jesus after the crucifixion (John 19:38-42). In the end, Nicodemus experienced God in his heart.

Jesus was telling them that the Kingdom of God will come to you if you have allowed God to be sovereign in your life. It's a radical way of being. It is the state of being saturated and consumed by God, literally becoming the dwelling place of God's Kingdom so that what comes out of us is in accord with the heart of God. The Kingdom of God is totally different than what people had expected during the time of Jesus... and in our present time. It is not a political regime but one of heaven on earth. It is counter-culture that breaks tradition and requires a new way of thinking and living. It is uncommon; it is mysterious and beyond what is normal. It calls for reformation and transformation of society. It is a force that cannot be thwarted, manipulated and suppressed. It is beyond powerful but yet it is gentle; it is superlative over everything and yet not controlling. The Kingdom cannot be contained and defined by human minds. It is the invasion of God Himself in our midst. It requires radical living, renovation of the heart, and renewal of the mind that transcends our entire being. Hence it is foreign to our forefathers and, more than 2,000 years later, in our society.

We can then conclude that the Kingdom would mean the kingship of God in our world, in our lives. One may also say the sovereignty, rule and the dominion of God.

## Kingdom way of living

The disciples saw Jesus model the new way of living. They were to pray for their enemies and love those who were unlovable. In the Old Testament, people were forbidden to touch the lepers and the unclean because they would be unclean themselves. On the contrary, Jesus came to earth and He touched the unclean and the sick and He healed them! Jesus expected the disciples not just to learn and to observe Him but to put His teachings into practice in their everyday lives. They were to *experience* Kingdom living.

On many occasions, Jesus let His disciples do the things themselves, such as when He sent the 72 to minister to every town and place He was about to go. Also at the feeding of the 5,000, the disciples experienced the multiplication of bread through their own hands. Then the disciples came back joyfully; it was hard for them to believe what they were able to do. Luke 10:17-19 says, *The seventy-two returned with joy and said, "Lord, even the demons submit to us in your name." He replied, "I saw Satan fall like lightning from heaven. I have given you authority to trample on snakes and scorpions and to overcome all the power of the enemy; nothing will harm you."* Jesus said that believers have been given authority to overpower *all* the authority and power of the enemy. I bet the 72 couldn't wait for the next time Jesus would tell them to do it again!

It is fascinating to see how Jesus taught His disciples and those who opposed Him. One day, Jesus returned to the Mount of Olives, His favorite place. Many historical events occurred there during Old and New Testament times. While Jesus was speaking, the two religious groups of the day—the teachers of the law and the Pharisees—interrupted his teaching. They pushed a woman caught in adultery into the middle of the crowd and in front of Jesus. They quoted the Book of the Law that the woman should be stoned. They asked Him what He would do so they could trap Him. (Imagine if you were teaching about God or leading a meeting when suddenly two groups of people from two different sects came throwing a prostitute in front of you and then used Scripture to see what you would do.) Instead of answering them, Jesus stooped down and wrote something on the ground with His fingers. But they kept demanding an answer from Him. He stood up and said, *"All right, but let the one who has never sinned throw the first stone"* (John 8:1-11, NLT). They slipped away one by one, beginning with the oldest. You can only imagine how the two groups felt in front of a crowd of people.

One of my friends, Donna, works at a hospital. She is an RN with a mission. Her personal mission is to bring the love of Jesus to every patient that she comes in contact with. She prays for them and shares the Bible with them. She expects miracles and healings at her workplace. She talks to the doctors about Jesus and she invites them to go to church with her or to any Bible-believing church. She brings encouragement to her patients in practical ways. She even tries to involve her co-workers in some of the community services she does.

Outside of her job, she leads worship at different churches and ministries; she walks the streets to reach out to the down-trodden. She prays for people wherever she goes. She gives generously to others. Donna goes to different Christian trainings and conferences because she hungers for what God has for her and for others.

During one of the Super Bowl outreaches we had in 2012, she prayed for a person who had been limping on her left leg. She and another friend of mine, Bill, stooped down in the middle of thousands of people, reached to the person's foot and commanded the foot to be healed in Jesus' name! The person that they were praying for was not a believer. She felt that her foot was healed and she later received Jesus Christ as her Lord and Savior!

Merlin with his friend Pferron at Super Bowl XLVI Indianapolis.

Volunteers Donna and Bill praying for a lady in Super Bowl XLVI Village.

That same night, I happened to have a conversation with a few men who had some alcoholic drinks. Donna joined the conversation, asked a few questions and we ended up praying for them. I thought we were done, but then Donna felt like asking one of the men if he liked cars. Right in front of my eyes, I saw this man's physical appearance immediately change from being tipsy to sober. He said that he was just sharing with his friends moments before that he would like to work on cars. He had been contemplating opening a business buying and selling cars. Because of the special knowledge the Lord had given Donna about this man, he knew he was encountering the real deal and he received Jesus to be the Lord of his life that same night.

Donna is an example of living out the Kingdom of God every day. It means following the teachings of Jesus and applying them in every aspect of your life. She is an example of a mature Christian who lives out her faith. I don't know about you, but to me it's better to be in the game rather than a spectator. As the apostle Paul said in 1 Corinthians 4:20, *"For the kingdom of God is not a matter of talk but of power."*

## Breaking through in the Kingdom

In this section, we will look at a few things that introduce us to the Kingdom. As mentioned earlier, the Kingdom is infinitely broad. We will attempt to uncover a few of the human tendencies that can block us from what God has for us. Even one of the most influential and super-educated people in the New Testament was blinded by the world's ways from breaking through in the Kingdom—Saul, later known as the apostle Paul.

Jesus expects us to establish His realm or His rule here on earth. He taught us about Kingdom values and principles when He proclaimed them during the Sermon on the Mount. Meanwhile, the teachers of the law and the Pharisees had been after Jesus, condemning Him for disregarding the law and accusing Him many times as a blasphemer. In Matthew 5, Jesus taught about the attitudes of the heart. Jesus covered six Old Testament laws and explained them in new ways that baffled even the teachers of the law. In a simple but unfamiliar way, Jesus told them that He honors the law; He came to fulfill it. Jesus helped the people learn the law, love it, understand it in a new way, and live it. Jesus shed light on the topics so that listeners could have a glimpse of the Kingdom He was ushering in.

On many occasions, Jesus exposed the militant adherence to tradition that led people to bondage rather than freedom. We should obey the law not out of fear but out of love for God and for others. He spoke about the shallowness of external righteousness that hid wrong motivations and pride deep in people's hearts. The leaders, instead of leading people to holiness, led them down the wrong path, one that fosters control and selfish ambition. Their religion was dry ritual rather than a flowing and loving Spirit-filled relationship. We know that these things are still true in our society! However, the holy discontent is spreading in our community, starting with our churches. You can see it, smell it and sense it. The face of the Church is changing. The Spirit of Truth is reviving.

As an apostle of Christ, Paul studied spiritual theories and principles. He was the cream of the crop. Reared in a Jewish home, educated under strict Jewish laws and regarded outstanding over most of his fellow Pharisees, Paul's credentials would surpass many PhDs' and conference speakers of our days! But after he studied the Scripture and became skilled at it, he persecuted the early Christians. The Book of Acts states that Paul, before his conversion, became too religious. Just as he did with Paul, satan can put blinders on people's eyes and hearts even after studying the Scripture. We only have to look so far to see that this is still the case in our culture. We become too religious and we miss God's heart.

The face of the Church is changing. The Spirit of Truth is reviving.

---

## Knowledge without relationship is empty

For example, look at the Pharisees and Sadducees and the teachers of the law—they studied about the coming Messiah but when the Messiah came, they did not recognize Him. However, the demoniacs, the prostitutes and the "unclean" recognized Jesus right away. *When he saw Jesus from a distance, he ran and fell on his knees in front of him. He shouted at the top of his voice, "What do you want with me, Jesus, Son of the Most High God?"* (Mark 5:6).

The Kingdom is more than just information—it's about conversion. For many years, I thought I was a Christian but I still lived like a non-believer. I had the information about God but my heart was not converted. I grew up in the Philippines where my mother taught me to go to church on a regular basis. So, I thought I was a Christian. My relatives and friends went to church a few times a week so I grew up to be a churchgoer. Later, I found out that a churchgoer is not necessarily a Christian.

In my early twenties, I moved to the U.S. Since I was a little boy, I always dreamed of living in the U.S. In my early twenties, that dream became a reality. I realized that God answered my prayer and I was so thankful. I started reading my Bible again regularly, but after a few months I indulged myself in the ways of the world. After a year in the states, I got married and moved to Indianapolis. My wife and I went to a church on a weekly basis. I got baptized there. We got involved in the children's ministry and a Bible study group for several years. But the cravings of my sinful heart crept in again; I became unfaithful. Our 11 years of marriage ended up in divorce. I committed sin and reaped the consequences of it. I did not turn from sin to Christ. I had the information in my head about God and His commandments but my heart was not converted. Jesus said in Mark 7:21-22, *"For it is from within, out of a person's heart, that evil thoughts come—sexual immorality, theft, murder, adultery, greed, malice, deceit, lewdness, envy, slander, arrogance and folly."* The Kingdom was not real in my heart. It was just head knowledge, stagnant and no life.

## God wants us to move from knowledge to relationship.

Romans 14:10 says, *How, then, can they call on the one they have not believed in?* It is necessary to have knowledge of the teachings, the life and the works of Christ, but it is not enough. In marriage, it takes more than knowledge about our spouse. It would help to know the love language, food, activities, habits, his/her past and countless other things. However, there's no relationship in just knowing her/him. Jesus said, *"Remain in me, as I also remain in you. No branch can bear fruit by itself; it must remain in the vine. Neither can you bear fruit unless you remain in me. I am the vine; you are the branches. If you remain in me and I in you, you will bear much fruit; apart from me you can do nothing"* (John 15:4-5). Jesus describes a relationship with Him that is intimately connected at all times with Him. It is His desire that we always be in relationship with him, no matter what. His promise is that we will produce the heavenly fruits here on earth that come only through Him. How futile it is to expect to produce spiritual fruits through worldly ways.

In a marriage, we do life together; it is active and participatory. Relationship is the bond that holds the marriage together. It is the same with any relationships, with our friends, parents or neighbors. The same is true of God—it is not enough to just have knowledge about Him. It is not even enough if we do good deeds to gain favor with God and to attract the attention of men. We can be so educated in theology and religious philosophies but if we do not have relationship with God, then we become like the Pharisees and the Sadducees who could quote the Scriptures by memory but missed Christ even when He was standing right in front of them. It is my desire to know Him more and deepen my relationship with Him every day of my life.

## Don't just learn it—experience it!

In 2006, we launched one of our ministry trainings called, "Don't Just Learn It—Experience It!" After classroom training, we would send our attendees out in the streets to apply what they had learned. Most of the time, we learn more by doing. Experience is a great teacher.

In Mark 5:25-34, there was a woman who had been suffering from constant bleeding for 12 years. She spent all her money on doctors' bills but it only got worse. She had heard about Jesus and found out that He would be passing by her town. However,

Jesus attracted so many people that it was very hard for her to get to Him. In her desperation, she tried to get closer to Jesus to touch even the hem of His garment. As soon as she touched His garment, she got healed right at that moment. She knelt before Jesus and told Him what happened. Out of her knowledge of Jesus, she took action and she experienced the power of God moving in her!

In 2004, my wife Annie and I faced a big challenge—we both lost our jobs within three months of each other. At that time, I still had my child support obligations and we had some credit card bills on top of our monthly utility bills. We did not even have any savings. We had just moved to a 784 square foot apartment owned by our friend. It was difficult to find jobs at that time.

Somehow, I had peace that everything would be alright. I started to read Christian books, Bible references and commentaries. I even started running on a regular basis while listening to my previous church leadership classes. My trust in God was supported by my intellect and head knowledge. However, doubt crept in whenever I received negative responses from potential employers and my head knowledge of God would quickly disappear. But my faith would rise up again every time I read the promises in the Bible and received encouragement from friends. At about this time, my wife got a job after three months of being unemployed. Deep inside me, I knew I would experience God in a tangible way.

One day, I received an offer. It was a decent offer; however, I found out I would be working 10 hours a day as a salesperson with a base salary plus commission. After conferring with my wife, I turned it down because it would interfere with my volunteer work at my church and I would not be able to participate in some of the outreaches that are near and dear to me. So I began speaking to the Lord about this. I asked for three specific things: To work part time in a ministry, to be my own boss so I can have flexible hours for ministry, and a specific amount of income.

The very day I ran out of unemployment benefits, I received a call from a friend of mine who offered me a consulting job with his client paying me the exact amount of income I had prayed for previously. This job had flexible hours, and I got to work at home and was still able to fulfill my volunteer commitment with my church. Because of the flexibility of this business, I was offered a part-time position as outreach pastor for my church and I was able to start an amazing ministry that mobilizes thousands of volunteers on a yearly basis. I experienced God and His character in a mighty way! I learned far more about God through my personal experience with Him than I did in the many months of reading books about Him. In my new consulting job I worked fewer hours and with better pay than I would have gotten in the job I turned down. This particular time of my life was instrumental in equipping me to start a ministry.

## Tangible reality of the sovereignty of God

Here's another way to put it: *You're here to be light, bringing out the God-colors in the world. God is not a secret to be kept. We're going public with this, as public as a city on a hill. If I make you light-bearers, you don't think I'm going to hide you under a bucket, do you? I'm putting you on a light stand. Now that I've put you there on a hilltop, on a light stand—shine! Keep open house; be generous with your lives. By opening up to others, you'll prompt people to open up with God, this generous Father in heaven* (Matthew 5:14-16, The Message).

The Kingdom of God is not just an inward resolve for followers of Christ but should be expressed in practical ways. Jesus healed the sick, fed the hungry and released those in captivity. Jesus told His followers not only to operate in the Kingdom but also to model it to others, to teach others. This is not easy. We are operating in a society that endorses sin and can get away with it. Christians are the minority and we are in conflict with the majority. One needs only to observe the entertainment world that promotes sex, drugs and violence. Movies, TV shows, books and the like promote the underworld and they make lots of money. Most reality shows are about degrading women and making men look like fools; the more profanity and evil, the better. Why would all these things thrive? Have we become immune to the world's way that we forget whose we are?

That's why Jesus said to bring the light into this dark world, to model His teachings. However, we have to be careful not to base our righteousness solely upon outward obedience. Doing good things does not entitle us entrance into the coming Kingdom. As mentioned earlier, our actions are fruits of our inner motivation that comes from our character. It begins with our heart and our relationship with Him.

The Kingdom of God is not just an inward resolve for followers of Christ but should be expressed in practical ways.

Jesus provided us practical teachings on human conduct and ethics. He was more interested in people rather than rules and tradition. He said in Matthew 15:6, *"Thus you nullify the word of God for the sake of your tradition."* Jesus' attention was on the quality of life, the well being of an individual rather than power and control. He demonstrated the power of God out of love and compassion instead of being prideful and arrogant. Ironically, the most influential people in our history are those who have big hearts rather than those who have big pockets and large bank accounts.

The Kingdom comes to our cities when we welcome the heavenliness and when we act under the reign of God. As mentioned earlier, this can be challenging because the Kingdom is about the end times and the eternal. We know that Jesus brought the Kingdom and has broken through in our present time; in other words, the eternal has invaded the temporal. This creates tension. It is the collision of the natural and the supernatural, the temporal and the eternal. The impact between the physical and the spiritual and the effect of two different kingdoms will shatter our worldview and tradition. There will be opposition, theological debates, philosophical discussions and division among friends and families. You will be going against the grain. You will be misinterpreted because His ways are not the world's way. Don't be surprised when you operate in the Kingdom principles and are ridiculed and judged. Jesus said *"my Kingdom is not of this world"* (John 18:36). However, these are challenges that will only strengthen our faith in Him. Don't try to logically explain and theoretically debate the Kingdom principles and values. The obvious teachings are the Sermon on the Mount (Matthew 5-7), the Golden Rule, (Luke 6:27-31), and the parable of the Good Samaritan (Luke 10:30-37).

A few testimonies come to mind that some of our volunteers shared with me of their experiences during an FHL Week (a week of missions which I will describe later):

"A man at the restaurant couldn't believe that we wanted to clean their toilets for them. He kept asking what the catch was and it was awesome to see his reaction when we assured him that it was free."

"My sons were talking with someone who was sad about her son's death. They asked for someone else to come and help. When I came up she shared her story with me, and I was aware of her drinking. She knew she needed God but shared with me her anger at Him. We prayed; she was overwhelmed that someone came to her and visited with her. She also said she wanted to come to church."

"One gentleman asked me, 'What company are you advertising for?' when we were passing out free water. I answered that we were just sharing God's love through acts of kindness. His face lit up and he answered, 'Wish more people would do that!'"

The Kingdom ways are different than the world's ways (Hebrews 3:10).

## The Holy Spirit, our advocate

Going against the grain, minority, weird, etc.—that's what we've signed up for if we are the followers of Christ. How can we overcome the world then? We are the minority and the world thinks we are going the wrong direction. If we are to do the ministry God had given us, we need our best friend—the Holy Spirit. God has given us access to heavenly resources and authority through the Holy Spirit who is at work in us. The Holy Spirit comes in power from above and enables believers to be conduits of God's blessings. We become God's ambassadors and His constituents here on earth through the Holy Spirit. How cool is that!

In the Old Testament, the Spirit of God comes upon people with special assignments from God. For example, King Saul, King David and Samson, all of them were chosen to fulfill particular positions from God. All of them filled particular offices from God and Spirit-endowed them for their work. However, the Spirit leaves people when they sin against God (1 Samuel 16:14, Judges 14:6 and 16:20). Even David asked God not to take away His Spirit (Psalm 51:11).

In the New Testament period, the Holy Spirit did not just come upon people but dwelt in them permanently. *And I will ask the Father, and he will give you another advocate to help you and be with you forever— the Spirit of truth. The world cannot accept him, because it neither sees him nor knows him. But you know him, for he lives with you and will be in you* (John 14:16-17). The Scripture is clear to point out that the Holy Spirit lives forever in all of us—not just the official leaders—if we are followers of Christ.

The term "advocate" was used only by the apostle John, which came from a Greek word *Paracletos*, meaning "called alongside to assist." It could also be translated comforter, counselor or encourager. One commentary states, "The Holy Spirit does work not instead of us or in spite of us but in us and through us." The Spirit works in our hearts to enable us to impart "streams of living water" to others. "*Whoever believes in me, as Scripture has said, rivers of living water will flow from within them"* (John 7:38). John added his commentary on verse 39, *"By this he meant the Spirit, whom those who believed in him were later to receive. Up to that time the Spirit had not been given, since Jesus had not yet been glorified."* Since the Spirit lives in us and He is our advocate, we can accomplish anything God calls us to do. That is why it is very important to know what God had called us to do. The will of God will be fulfilled in us if we respond to Him. Once we receive the Holy Spirit, we enter into newness of life. New possibilities and endless horizons are before us. In fact, the impossibilities of the world will become our normal way of life. Miracles will be an everyday occurrence and should be expected when the Spirit of God works as our advocate.

Let's detour here for a few moments: If He lives in us and we are the Body of Christ, then why are we questioning supernatural healing? If the Advocate works in us, then why do we doubt that He can raise the dead through us? Why do we question that miracles, signs and wonders are to be expected in our everyday lives? Maybe most of us assume that the Holy Spirit would not allow us to do the things that Jesus did because our finite minds cannot explain them. Do we tend to follow the worldview and reason like the Pharisees did during the time of Jesus? Consider this: Jesus said that the same Spirit who lived in Him while He was here on earth is the very same One who is now living in us and still capable of doing the things that He did through Jesus—and even greater things! Is He limited now because He lives in us? Are we limiting the Advocate's work through us and thereby affecting the next generation by hindering the advancement of the Kingdom of God? Is this the same reason why Jesus said in Mathew 23:24, *"You blind guides!..."*

The Books of Matthew, Mark and Luke attribute the birth of Jesus to the creative power of the Holy Spirit. Jesus launched His ministry after He was baptized with the Holy Spirit and the Gospels agree that Jesus was endowed by the Spirit to fulfill His messianic mission. Jesus was bestowing on His disciples the same Spirit that had descended on Him at His baptism and filled Him during His ministry. He endows them with the Spirit because He is sending His disciples into the world to continue His mission for which He was sent.[4]

Why do we question that miracles, signs and wonders are to be expected in our everyday lives?

We can have the fellowship of the Holy Spirit and we can also grieve Him because He is a person (2 Cor. 13:14; Eph 4:30). The Holy Spirit has many gifts for those who believe in Jesus (1 Cor. 12). On one occasion, while he was eating with them, he gave them this command: *"Do not leave Jerusalem, but wait for the gift my Father promised, which you have heard me speak about. For John baptized with water, but in a few days you will be baptized with the Holy Spirit"* (Acts 1:4-5).

After we receive the Holy Spirit, we need to be filled by Him over and over again. *After they prayed, the place where they were meeting was shaken. And they were all filled with the Holy Spirit and spoke the word of God boldly* (Acts 4:31).

---

4    See G.E. Ladd, A Theology of the New Testament, 323-325

In the Book of Acts, the disciples experienced being filled by the Spirit over and over again.

## Creative power within us

During the second year of Faith Hope and Love, I was prompted by the Holy Spirit to launch our ministry big time. The other pastors who partnered with me the previous year were smiling at my big dream and me. They knew I still owed a few hundred dollars from the first year of outreach. I pursued what I believed God wanted to do.

The plan was to have a large Christian concert at Conseco Fieldhouse, which was the home of the Indiana NBA team. Many people said it wasn't going to happen since it would cost thousands of dollars to rent the place plus a lot more money to bring nationally known Christian bands and their equipment shipment and accommodations. Never did I think there were so many things I had to do to put together a concert, from renting the venue, booking the band, coordinating with many groups of people, installing the sound system, marketing and selling tickets. Plus I had to find sponsors and partners to make a two-hour concert possible. In addition to the concert, I also planned to have a family-style festival in the parking lot outside the arena. This outside event involved children's games, selling our t-shirts and some giveaways. By the way, this event was scheduled to happen after the weeklong citywide local missions that involve 1,200-plus volunteers, more than 50 projects and services, and about 50 organizations—all ran by volunteers with no money for the project. This was over my head! I continued to pray, asking the Holy Spirit to fill me once again and to be my Advocate.

I did not know anyone at the Fieldhouse and did not know how to start. After few days passed, a friend of mine invited me to a lunch meeting for an organization that was new to all of us. There were about 30 people there and I sat toward the middle of the room next to a person who was wearing a nice suit. Soon the meeting started and I found out that the person next to me was one of the presenters. He was the sales manager for the Fieldhouse! I spoke with him right after the meeting and within a few days, I visited him at the Fieldhouse to discuss the event in the summer. After a few minutes of speaking with him and his assistant, we agreed to meet with his boss.

That same week, I drafted my proposal with 24 requests including: FHL will not put out any money but will receive a certain percentage of the ticket sales, they (Fieldhouse) will pay for the band, they prepare the venue and any musical setup, free meals and t-shirt with any ticket purchase, several suite rooms for our special guests, advertising on their Jumbotron and media a few weeks before the event. I sent the proposal to my contact, who in turn passed it to his boss.

After a few days, I met with him, his assistant and his boss. His boss, the VP, was very cold and I could tell her eyes were sizing me up. Her first words were, "What do you want?" I presented my plan and after 15 minutes, a miracle just happened in front of my eyes—the VP changed her attitude toward me and said, "We can do this together." We shook hands afterward and later that week, I signed the agreement. In the end, we were handed a donation of more than $1,100 from Conseco Fieldhouse with no money invested on my part! I left praising God for what He had done. I know it was not my proposal since all the 24 demands were in favor of our organization.

Conseco Fieldhouse presents check to
Faith Hope & Love.

After that week, I was on top of the mountain and my faith was lifted up so high, I felt I could do anything with the help of the Holy Spirit. I was never the same afterward. I started to dream bigger and got connected with influential people of the city. The Mayor of Indianapolis plus nine other mayors actually issued a proclamation in their own cities recognizing the last full week of July to be FHL Week, a weeklong mission in local neighborhoods.

The Holy Spirit enables us to be miracle workers and history makers. He can raise us up above any challenge. *We will soar on wings like eagles; we will run and not grow weary, we will walk and not be faint.* He can breathe life on mere plans and we can see the hands of God work out the details to bring it to reality. We can see in the physical what we have conceived in the spiritual. We become the hands of God and see "His way of doing things." We can co-labor with His Spirit and see the heavenly ways become common in our world. Indeed, heaven invades our world when we partner with the Holy Spirit. He can work through our ministries as we proclaim the lordship of Jesus. Come, Holy Spirit.

Through us, God is expanding His sovereignty over our neighborhoods. We bring the Kingdom of Heaven to earth through the loving demonstration of power and authority from God.

More than two years ago, I was invited to speak at a small Hispanic church. Some of the members of our team go with me whenever I speak so they can minister to the congregation as well. That morning, we had some challenges setting up the video and sound system, which delayed the start time of the service. We started worship with a few people joining the singing and worshipping. Then, we started the bilingual service. Toward the end of the message, I felt the Holy Spirit coming in power. The people's outward appearance and facial expressions changed. I was prompted to ask for those who had not accepted Jesus as their Lord and Savior. To my amazement, 12 people walked to the front and stood there until someone prayed for them. The pastor of the church and his wife were astonished to see that the people who came forward had been going to their church for quite some time. Our team prayed for all of them and led them to receive Jesus as their Savior. At the end of the service, we blessed the pastor and his wife. I saw the power of the Holy Spirit over my daughter as she was sitting on the floor weeping. The "rule of God" was experienced in that church that Sunday morning. Let your Kingdom come!

We bring the Kingdom of Heaven to earth through the loving demonstration of power and authority from God.

We are created in the image of God. Our real identity will be recognized by the works we do.

A few years ago, I was having a meeting with some of our leaders in our conference room when I heard someone enter the office. I greeted a young college student who wanted to volunteer for our ministry. She saw our advertising on their university ListServ. The rest of our leadership team was looking at me to see what my reaction would be. Leila, the girl who was applying for a volunteer job, was obviously a Muslim because of her Hijab (traditional head covering for Muslin women). Without hesitation, I had her fill out our volunteer form and showed her our office. Later, I showed her some work she could do. I was happy that volunteers from other religions feel safe to volunteer and would not worry about being judged or persecuted.

Muslim volunteers serving at food pantry.

The following week, Leila came back to volunteer again. My curiosity prompted me to ask her why she continued to volunteer for our ministry. She answered without hesitation, "You guys do worthwhile services for the hungry. You are reaching out to them through your food pantry." I smiled at her as she did some paperwork. Later, I invited her to serve at one of our food pantry sites. She smiled and excitedly said that she has some friends who might volunteer as well. I prayed and asked the Holy Spirit to lead the upcoming pantry.

We release His power into our city and change the spiritual and physical atmosphere through our testimonies.

———

At the food pantry, we start by bagging the groceries ahead of time. I assigned Leila and her nine friends to bagging the groceries and serving hot soup for the clients. It was a bold move for me to let them volunteer with us since the neighborhood knows we are a Christian organization. Plus, I cannot control what the other volunteers and the Christian clients would say; there was the possibility that the Muslim students could be judged or ill-treated by others. I noticed that the line was getting long and the building was getting full. Our procedure is to pray with our volunteers before we start any of our pantries. We always invite everyone to join us in thanking the Lord for His provision and most of the time, all of them join us. As I started to pray, I noticed that the Muslims stayed and I ended the prayer, "In the name of Jesus, amen." Many people welcomed the students and everyone was blessed that day! When the Pharisees saw this, they asked his disciples, "Why does your teacher eat with tax collectors and sinners?" On hearing this, Jesus said, "It is not the healthy who need a doctor, but the sick. But go and learn what this means: 'I desire mercy, not sacrifice.' For I have not come to call the righteous, but sinners" (Matthew 9:11-13).

We release His power into our city and change the spiritual and physical atmosphere through our testimonies. I will give you the keys of the kingdom of heaven; whatever you bind on earth will be bound in heaven, and whatever you loose on earth will be loosed in heaven (Matthew 16:19). Last year (2011) in Indianapolis we experienced an extremely hot summer. Our ministry's largest event, FHL Week - Mission Trip in your Own Backyard, is always held during the last full week of July. It is a weeklong local mission in central Indiana that mobilizes more than 1,000 volunteers doing numerous projects and services in different communities. We start the week with a Prayer Celebration at the heart of downtown Indianapolis. That year, we decided to add a special dance by more than 240 participants. After the dance, they would leave their shoes on the street (where they dance), which will be given to the homeless through a foot washing outreach at the end of the week. We always start the celebration at 3 p.m. By noon, the temperature was already in the 90s and one of our volunteers at another site was brought to a hospital because of heat exhaustion.

A storm was lurking just before the Prayer Celebration.

Shoes were left on a wet street after the dance. Rain cooled down the asphalt just before the dance.

That month had been very dry; however, that particular day it was expected to rain. I had been interceding in prayer for several days for this event that the weather would be cooler than normal and with just short rain showers before the event to cool down with some gentle wind. This event is always outdoors and it has rained the past two years during the event. By 2 p.m., the temperature index was over 100 degrees with high humidity. I saw some people pour water on their heads to cool down. Donna, our worship leader, was already getting sick; they just started to do a sound check. The city already gave us warning of the heat that day. They said that the asphalt street (the place where the dancers would dance) would be more than 10 degrees hotter than the air temperature. How would the dancers dance on the hot asphalt, let alone taking off their shoes and walk back to the grassy area? How about the sound systems and the band members?

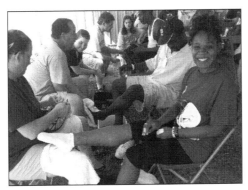

Shoes that were collected at the dance were given to those in need.

Suddenly, I saw dark clouds starting to form in the sky. The wind picked up and I saw the concerned look from our volunteers and the public. I thought to myself, "Not again!" While I was looking at the sky a young man tapped me on

my shoulder and said, "It's not going to rain, is it?" I told him
no. Within 10 minutes I felt the first drop of rain and the cool
wind started to pick up. Donna continued to lead the band in
worship. I was determined to put my faith into action in front
of Indianapolis. I was prompted by the Holy Spirit to command
the atmosphere to stop raining and to cool down. I have never
done this before, and I was in front of hundreds of people in a
public place. It is easier to practice your faith in the confinement
of a church or a friendly environment than in a public place with
many strangers.

I gathered myself, went to the stage and took the microphone.
I asked everyone for his/her attention. I quoted Romans 14:17:
"*For the kingdom of God is not a matter of eating and drinking,
but of righteousness, peace and joy in the Holy Spirit.*" I
encouraged everyone to agree with me to release righteousness,
peace and joy in the Holy Spirit so we can release the Kingdom
right then and there. Then, I told them the story when Jesus
commanded the storm to calm down. I asked them again to agree
with me that the atmosphere would change at my command in
the name of Jesus. By this time, I was already getting wet. The
cool wind started to blow harder and blew our tents away. It was
going to storm. With a commanding voice, I said, "I command
you, rain, to stop and the wind to calm down!" I stepped down
off the stage but the light rain continued and the wind was even
stronger. We had to shut down our sound system and cover all
our equipment. I saw the clouds moving as I was watching the
sky.

Suddenly, I felt a tap on my shoulder again. It was the same
young man and he said, "I thought you said that the rain will
stop?" I told him to just watch. I continued to walk around
while praying. One of our partnering ministry leaders showed

me the cloud activity on the weather application on his smart phone. The cloud was circling around away from our area. Within five minutes the rain stopped, but the gentle cool wind continued. I looked at the sky; it was still somewhat cloudy but not dark anymore. The air temperature cooled down by more than 10 degrees and the asphalt street immediately dried up but it cooled down a lot. We started at 3 p.m. with cooler weather. Many other volunteers showed up after we started because the strong wind and the downpour had hampered them. They said that there were even several accidents on the highway because of the extreme weather and downpour. They thought that the event would be cancelled.

We had the cool weather the rest of the celebration; most of the people in the park were amazed at what just happened. Then I remembered what I had been praying a few days before the event: "Lord, it would be great to have cooler than normal weather, with gentle wind; let it rain a little bit if that's what it takes to cool things down." My faith was tested and the Holy Spirit honored our prayers and our boldness for Him. It was a display of His power working in those who believe in Him. It was a testimony of His faithfulness in front of hundreds of people. It was a display of the Kingdom of God in our midst, a testimony that baffled my mind, and I saw the demonstration of His power in us.

## QUESTIONS FOR STUDY

1.  It is our privilege to co-labor with Christ. Define co-labor and give 5 practical examples that can be done within a week, a month in your own neighborhood.

    _____

    _____

    _____

    _____

2.  What would your neighborhood look like if you could say, "The Kingdom of God is here"?

    _____

    _____

    _____

    _____

3.  Formulate an empowering question that would move people to action.

    _____

    _____

    _____

    _____

4.  Read Genesis 28. What does the ladder represent? Jacob's accommodation that night was a less than comfortable motel, but he had the most wonderful dream that changed the course of his life and the history of the world. Why do you think God chose that particular place and that specific night to communicate with him?

    _____

    _____

    _____

    _____

5.  Write about a time in your life when God spoke to you. What was your situation and how did it affect your life?

    _____

    _____

    _____

    _____

6.  Which part of "The Setup" section (page 15) can you relate to?

    _____

    _____

    _____

    _____

7. Read John 1:43-50. Write about a time in your life when God set you up for the next revelation.

_____

_____

_____

_____

8. Read Ephesians 2:6-10. What does "seated us with him in the heavenly realms" mean? Verse 10 states, "which God prepared in advance for us to do." Refer to the "It couldn't be me" section on page 21—have you experienced "doing good" without even thinking about it?

_____

_____

_____

_____

9. What is your understanding of the Kingdom of God? What action would you take in order to experience the Kingdom of God personally?

_____

_____

_____

_____

10. Read Romans 14:17-18. Apostle Paul was saying that it's not the external things that matter but a person's motivation, such as their spiritual realities expressed outwardly. Give an example of a noble thing that you have done but with an unrighteous motivation.

_____

_____

_____

_____


11. Read Luke 17:20-21. What does "the Kingdom of God is in your midst" mean to you? Based on your answer, would it be impossible now to expect miracles, signs and wonders, healings, casting out demonic spirits, raising the dead and multiplying of fish and bread?

_____

_____

_____

_____

# PART TWO

# Signs of
## the Kingdom

And when he comes, he will open the eyes of the blind
and unplug the ears of the deaf.
The lame will leap like a deer,
and those who cannot speak will sing for joy!

—ISAIAH 35:5-6 NLT

D o you believe in miracles? How about the supernatural and the spiritual world? Is it possible that God heals the sick and the afflicted through His people? Would God use a mere human being to release people from demonic captivity? Does God speak to us now, and how? What do people mean when they pray "Use me, Lord; I want to be your hands and feet"? Is His presence tangible in our lives today? I have many questions, more than answers. Let's look at some recent real-life stories and some passages in the Bible.

In late summer of 2004, my wife Annie and I were still living in the 784 square foot apartment in the upper room of our friend Scott's house. I was leading a Bible study group with fellow believers, which was sometimes as many as 20 people. The apartment would be full of people every week, some new believers and some Christians for many years. We were studying the Book of Acts at that time. It's been our habit to pray for each other according to what we've learned after each class.

Our worship leader Moses (yes Moses!) led us in worship before we dove into the study and discussions. On this particular night, we were studying Chapter 2 about the disciples being filled with the Holy Spirit on the day of Pentecost. Somehow, I sensed something special was about to happen that night.

*Suddenly a sound like the blowing of a violent wind came from heaven and filled the whole house where they were sitting. They saw what seemed to be tongues of fire that separated and came to rest on each of them. All of them were filled with the Holy Spirit and began to speak in other tongues as the Spirit enabled them* (Acts 2:2-4).

After the study, we huddled together and invited His presence to fill the upper room where we were and to fill all of us with the Holy Spirit. We waited for God's response to our prayers; the room was very quiet. After a couple minutes, which seemed like a long time of silence, all the people in the room simultaneously opened their eyes in awe. Many of us felt that the room started to shake and the sensation of a breeze was also felt on our faces. We looked at each other with amazement and for a moment did not know what to do next. I did not know what to make of it, but it was real—not just for me but also for several other people. Suddenly, all of us started to pray in our own way, praising God for allowing us to feel His tangible presence. Our friend Scott, who owned the house, came running up the stairs to see what was going on because he felt the house shake! From that time on, we started to expect God to meet with us together on our Bible study nights. We actually could not wait until the following week to be together again to see how the Holy Spirit would move. Our prayers became more intimate and powerful.

Expecting God to show up without self-seeking motives but rather a sheer longing for relationship and reverence would apprehend God's Kingdom in our midst. It is a child-like anticipation or trust, a sense of knowing that the Creator loves to be with His children. Our intimate relationship with our Beloved captivates and moves His heart. As much as we want His presence is nothing compared with His desire to engage and to participate in our lives. This notion drove us further into seeking His presence. Our prayers became more intense and our worship evolved into deeper reverence and awe of Him. Our group discussions began to include the practical applications of the Bible teachings.

On another night, we were studying Chapter 3 where the apostles Peter and John heal the crippled beggar. We were still talking about the night when the Holy Spirit visited us. It seemed like our faith could move mountains that night. We had a member who had been limping due to a complication with one of her legs. She walked with a cane and someone had to push her up the stairs as she slowly and painfully climbed one step at a time to our apartment. After the Bible study, she asked our group to pray for her healing. We surrounded her and each one of us prayed for her; some people stooped down to lay their hands on the afflicted leg. After a few minutes, her face and demeanor changed. She started to laugh and clapped her hands. To everyone's surprise, she unexpectedly began to jump again and again. She walked back and forth while shouting, "I'm healed, I'm healed!" The entire room was filled with praises, glorifying God for what He had done.

We had our snack while talking about what just happened. We were again in awe of what God was doing in our group. When it was time to go, we were discreetly looking at our friend who was just healed to see if she could go down the stairs by herself. She looked at us as if she was saying, "Look at me," and started to go down the stairs all by herself. She was praising God as she went down, exhilarated and full of energy! We followed her to her car, which was about half a block from the door of our apartment (our group filled the small street in front of our apartment). She was still shouting on the street, threw her cane and started to dance. She was like a little girl who just received her favorite gift on a Christmas morning. Indeed she was! She received a gift from our Father.

*Peter looked straight at him, as did John. Then Peter said, "Look at us!" So the man gave them his attention, expecting to get something from them. Then Peter said, "Silver or gold I do not have, but what I do have I give you. In the name of Jesus Christ of Nazareth, walk." Taking him by the right hand, he helped him up, and instantly the man's feet and ankles became strong. He jumped to his feet and began to walk. Then he went with them into the temple courts, walking and jumping, and praising God (Acts 3:4-8).*

Were these incidents signs of the Kingdom that Jesus inaugurated 2,000 years ago? Were these occurrences figments of our imagination or just coincidence? Let's look at some of the Scriptures together.

## Rediscovering the Kingdom

Jesus introduced the Kingdom of God when He came to earth more than 2,000 years ago. He taught about it through His words and actions. The Bible records that Jesus demonstrated the Kingdom more times than preaching it. He modeled the Kingdom to His disciples and they in turn modeled them to the next generation, and so on. But somehow, this very alive and active Kingdom power has been squelched or lost by believers through the generations. In this section, we will explore how our faith in doing the impossible has been suppressed, and how we can overcome this complacency to reawaken our beliefs and set our course again on operating in the Kingdom. We will rediscover Jesus' teachings through some stories in the Bible and see how we can apply these in our modern culture.

Sometimes the truth can get misdirected and even buried by the very tradition meant to celebrate it. Back in Jesus's time, and even today, traditions can easily become stumbling blocks if we do not question them.

In Jesus' time, some norms became patterns of living and then became religious beliefs that were imposed on the people. These traditions were used to judge and even condemn people. Every society needs rules and regulations; there needs to be laws of the land to govern a city or a nation. That's why since our early childhood we are taught to respect authority, or sometimes, as the saying goes, obey first then question later. However, human authorities are not perfect; although the intention is (usually) good, they need to be questioned.

I grew up in a town near the seashore. Swimming in the ocean was fun and my friends and I spent time at the public beach a few times a month. I learned to swim and dive at an early age. One day, my friends and I challenged each other to see who could reach the seashore first. I took a deep breath and started to swim as fast as I could. My little feet were like small propellers paddling fast. I closed my eyes and stroked harder. After a few minutes, I was sure I had won. However, I was off course a little bit. It took me longer to reach the beach even though I was going faster than my friends. I was doing all the right things except I deviated by just a tiny bit. I was going fast—in the wrong direction! Just like my incorrect compass, the way we enforce some of our religious traditions can affect our path like that. Just a slight difference off course can cause a huge deviation from the original intention. Applying this analogy to our leaders—if we know they are wrong, we have to show them the truth by applying course correction. That's what Jesus did!

Authorities come in different forms such as individuals, groups of people, or any kind of organization. A person's social status, educational background, position or wealth can be the basis for authority. In our modern day, talented people like those involved in the media, businesses, arts and entertainment develop ways to command authority or to gain followers. In Jesus' time, the two main authorities He frequently came in contact with were the Pharisees and the Sadducees, both religious leaders who demanded the respect of people. *"The teachers of the law and the Pharisees sit in Moses' seat. So you must be careful to do everything they tell you. But do not do what they do, for they do not practice what they preach"* (Matthew 23:2-3). Rediscovering the Kingdom takes intentionality and careful actions. We need to be mindful and observant.

## The Age to come

Many times in the Bible, we see Jesus teaching and correcting those in authoritative positions. He saw not only the needs of the people but their value and inherent nature. He did not look at people according to their social status but as children of God. His Father loves everyone no matter who they are and so does He. Nevertheless, many of those in authority had different kinds of lenses with which they viewed the world. Their standards and traditions were off course and self-serving. Sometimes they knew their rules were wrong but they wanted to keep their social status at the expense of another. A good example of a person in the Bible who wanted to keep his earthly status was Pontius Pilate. He was even warned by his wife, *"Don't have anything to do with that innocent man"* (Matthew 27:19), but he was afraid of what others would say. He was afraid to lose his friends, his authority and his money. The very thing that he was avoiding became his judgment. He lost not just his friends and cronies but his very soul.

In our present time, one does not need to look far to see certain individuals, groups of people or organizations who do not stand up for the right thing because they fear losing friends or their positions. This was also true in Jesus' time. *Yet at the same time many even among the leaders believed in him. But because of the Pharisees they would not openly acknowledge their faith for fear they would be put out of the synagogue* (John 12:42). They put more value in the system and status over a person. Because "it's been like that," they expected people to comply with their laws and traditions even though they were not relevant to the present time. Jesus was direct with those who just followed the traditions that were off course, obsolete or not serving the purpose anymore. *Then some Pharisees and teachers of the law came to Jesus from Jerusalem and asked, "Why do your disciples break the tradition of the elders? They don't wash their hands before they eat!" Jesus replied, "And why do you break the command of God for the sake of your tradition?"* (Matthew 15:1-3).

If we are not careful to respond to change and lose our
complacency, we may get run over—
and meanwhile lose something very valuable.

———

A biblical example of a misguided tradition is that of hand washing, which came from the law in the Old Testament for the ceremonial washing of hands before entering the tabernacle. This was passed down from one generation to another. It was adopted into their everyday life and eventually became a ritual of washing their hands in the morning and before every meal. Those who held this tradition were not trying to make their own rules but were simply following, without thinking, what was handed down to them from many generations ago. The problem was, it deviated from its original purpose and was given more importance than the people. It became part of their lives and somehow nobody ever questioned it. People even fought for it and the authorities dealt strong disapproval against any who opposed them.

We can apply this same situation in our churches and ministries today. You've heard the saying "If it's not broken, don't fix it." Well, what if the way we do things is not working as effectively as it should be? Our world is changing rapidly and if we are not careful to respond to change and lose our complacency, we may get run over—and meanwhile lose something very valuable.

Our technology, for example, is changing and improving every day. Some churches and ministries choose not to "go with the fad" but rather, stick with the old way of doing things. Not that they cannot afford it, but some say that the Internet is evil. This would be a misguided overstatement, a legalistic view. We know that inanimate objects cannot be evil. Therefore the Internet is not evil; it's how you *use* it that could be evil. It's up to you to respond to technology. God owns everything and He wants us to use them for His glory. We cannot leave the Internet to the devil to exploit it even more! We have to bring the rule of God over the Internet and technology. And we do this by opening our minds to the Spirit of God over man-contrived traditions and thought patterns.

## Social transformation

Jesus came not only to give us freedom from the bondage of sin but also to be "Christ-like" in the world. "We always bring people into our church every time we have an outreach. It's been like that since I've been here for 15 years," says one of the elders of a church. And yet, he asked why is it that their outreach is not yielding the same results it did 15 years ago. Their way of doing it served the original purpose back then, but was now far removed from the culture of their neighborhood. Many people had moved out and new people had moved in that changed the environment and the culture of the neighborhood.

Meanwhile, the leaders of the church unintentionally made life harder for the outreach team. They had strong trust in God and were faithfully committed to following the church tradition, but it actually stifled the people, both inside and outside of the church. Jesus affected the way people conducted their lives; he set people free from the confines of the law to love and to believe, to be healed and to live life fully. He discipled the religious people, the unclean and the demoniacs, the government leaders, educational gurus, the poor and the wealthy, and entire neighborhoods and communities.

### "The little town that could"

During FHL Week in 2009, I met a pastor of a small church in a very small community. She heard of the annual Mission Trip in your Own Backyard that happens every last full week of July in central Indiana. I found out from their "town historian" that this little town in the middle of cornfields had been a vibrant community some 80-plus years ago. They had a grocery store and other businesses in the area. They had a community that knew and cared for one another. However, due to people moving out, death, new people moving in and so forth, the neighborhood deteriorated throughout the years. In this town with less than 30 houses, now only a few of its people knew each other.

After my presentation, the pastor became interested and wanted to do an FHL mission week in her neighborhood. I encouraged her to have a town hall meeting to identify needs in their little community. After they met, she reported to me that they would not be able to participate because the church had no money for the projects; they needed $900 for a couple of projects they needed done.

Merlin having fun driving a backhoe.

Old home demolition at the
Little Town that Could.

Children's outreach at the end of the week.

I encouraged her to come to our FHL luncheon and invited her to share her needs. At the luncheon, she mentioned her project needs but that they didn't have the means to accomplish them. As the luncheon was ending, one church stepped up and donated $1,000 toward her little town's projects. Their previous town hall meeting had generated a long list of needs that would require even more resources. So I met with her leadership and encouraged them to talk to all the residents and neighboring town about the resources required. Armed with a story and an introduction letter from our organization, several of her townspeople went out to different potential partners and donors. One of the projects was to demolish three old houses and barns and another one was to cut big tree branches, and they needed a lift to reach the branches. At the next town meeting, the residents of this small town who did not know each other found out that they had resources right there in their own community. Friendships began to form as they came together and took pride in their town.

When I showed up for the actual FHL Week in her little town, I was surprised to see big machinery that looked like one of the machines in the movie *Transformers*. I learned they had a resident whose main business was to demolish old structures. He donated his machinery and labor for the demolition. A hardware company donated a lift and more than 100 people worked together the entire week. Most of the people in that neighborhood came out to volunteer for the Neighborhood Makeover. A husband and wife drove out their backhoe (I got to drive it, too!) to help in the demolition and to transport trash to dumpsters that were donated by the city. Some people were assigned to paint a house while the children went around the neighborhood with bottled water in a cart full of ice for all the volunteers.

At the end of the week, they had a neighborhood cookout. The children planted flowering plants in small pots that they painted during the week. They gave them to all the residents, along with a neighborhood telephone directory that they had created during the week. It was estimated that all the projects and services that week were valued at $60,000! They called their town, Elizaville, "The Little Town that Could!" God has scattered resources all around us; we just need to ask Him and the people around us for the resources we need.

**There's hope**

A local newspaper wrote an article for this year's FHL Week (2012) mentioning that many projects will be performed in central Indiana. Included in the article was the opportunity for a family to submit a project to be considered. Within a few days of publication, I received a call from a friend of a family who was in desperate need of a yard cleanup. I met with John at their house and found out that indeed, they are in desperate need of assistance. For the sake of privacy, we will call this couple John and Jane. Surrounding their trailer home are weeds taller than me, trash around the perimeter and a dilapidated detached garage. Overgrown tree branches clutter the yard. After a few days, I visited the family and met with Jane. She invited me into her house and I found out that she needs as much help inside. Their trailer home had only sub-flooring and there were a few holes in it. She needed a washer and other furniture. On top of all that, due to a vehicular accident in the mid '90s, Jane was paralyzed from the waist down, so she was not able to do much to attend to her children and her household.

I felt that we needed to help the family, but we did not have any monies for any projects at all. The idea for FHL Week is not only to mobilize the community but also to build a team to identify needs and resources in their own neighborhoods. FHL teaches people to walk by faith and to promote relationships over projects. This is done by gathering interested parties in meetings such as town hall, community, neighborhood and faith-based meetings. After weeks of planning and team building, the participants get to know each other. The result is trust that leads to relationship in which people can start to depend on one another. Once this happens, more things are done not for the sake of the projects, but for the sake of relationships and the community. The dynamics affect all sectors of a society including the family system, government and educational institutions, businesses, arts and entertainment, and the media.

Back to Jane's story... After a few days, I received a call from someone who had just moved to a city close to Indianapolis. She found out about FHL Week on the Internet and wanted to help, along with her children. However, as the week came close, she found out her husband had planned a nice vacation for their entire family during FHL Week. She felt really bad that they were not able to help so she stopped by our office and dropped off a check that funded some of the materials and paid labor for John and Jane's project. This shows how the Holy Spirit moves as we step out in faith.

Because of the desperate situation of Jane and her family, I named the project, "There's Hope." Soon the materials, tools, equipment and people we needed for the project started to come in. A dumpster company provided two large dumpsters. An electrical company provided three brand new ceiling fans and installed them as well. I later found out that a few days after installing the fans, the family's air conditioner broke. The month of July in 2012 was recorded as the hottest July ever in the history of Indiana. I can't imagine how hot it could be inside a trailer home during 100-plus degree weather. God knew what they needed at the right time.

The family had an acre of land that was full of limbs and other debris, which would require about 10 people to work seven hours per day for several days. I invited someone I had just recently met to the site; I asked him if he could help in some carpentry. He told me he was not a carpenter but he happened to have a Bobcat steer skid loader that could clear the land in an hour. By the end of the week, a project that did not have any money and no available volunteers to start with was accomplished, plus more than what was planned.

Justice, mercy and faithfulness are the
important qualities God is seeking.

---

## Un-"Natural Allies"

One might think that the religious leaders would be the natural allies of Jesus. After all, they read and studied the same Scripture. They had been waiting and observing the signs of the times for the Messiah all their lives. They had been anticipating His coming and they had been doing all the rituals to make themselves ready for His arrival. One might assume they would be the allies of Jesus, yet the opposite was true. Jesus had more conflicts with the Pharisees than with those who were branded as unclean and outcasts. The Bible records that most of their conflicts were about religious matters and social standing in the society. Jesus told them that the Kingdom does not come with their careful observation because the Kingdom is within them.

The religious leaders were more interested in the doctrines and theories but their hearts were not yielding to the Truth. That's why Jesus made a great analogy that they looked and sounded good but their inside was empty of the Truth: *"Woe to you, teachers of the law and Pharisees, you hypocrites! You give a tenth of your spices—mint, dill and cumin. But you have neglected the more important matters of the law—justice, mercy and faithfulness. You should have practiced the latter, without neglecting the former"* (Matthew 23:23).

The Pharisees majored in minors. They had rules for every minute area of life, while at the same time they had forgotten what was important—relationship. Usually, legalists are sticklers for details and the letter of the law, but blind to great principles... Justice, mercy and faithfulness are the important qualities God is seeking. Obeying the rules is no substitute. While paying attention to details, we must never lose our sense of priorities in spiritual matters.[5]

The teachers of the law were aristocrats and the Pharisees prided themselves on religious matters. Both groups had high social status and were known to separate themselves from the unclean and the outcast, to look down on the second-class citizens—inherited thinking that was handed down from generation to generation. They judged people who were not like them and those who did not fit their standards. If others challenged their essential teachings, perceived principles or doctrines, they didn't want anything to do with them. They were blinded whether intentionally or unintentionally by their religious systems. They became "professional religious people" and they failed to do what they were called to do. In addition, they failed to *understand* what they were called to do—to bring

---

5    Commentary taken from The Transformation Study Bible, NLT

the tangible love of God and to reach out to the sinners.

Three years ago I spoke to a group of pastors (most of them from the same denomination), encouraging them to work together in serving their neighborhoods. They were to identify needs, resources and to mobilize their congregation to serve. As I was speaking, I felt like I was in a courtroom in front of a jury to defend my case. After a short, tense presentation, I asked if there were any questions. One pastor asked me, "What is your doctrine?" That was the first time I heard that question in this type of setting. I smiled and kept silent. Then one of his colleagues stood up and said that it is not about doctrine but about expressing the love of God through serving people together. They continued the questions and answers amongst themselves while I took my seat. The pastor who had questioned me was more interested in little things over the more important thing—to serve those in need. He seemed to focus more on the religious stuff and missed the opportunity to bring the Body of Christ together in their community.

Jesus was known to hang out with the drunkards, the prostitutes and the unclean. These outcasts seemed attracted to Jesus and they were more open to listen to Him; conversely, they ran away from the religious people of the day. The "outcasts" grew up in a society where the religious leaders cared more about their status and their "doctrine" than caring for the people. It was normal for them to be treated as second-class people so they had no desire to be near the religious leaders. Their normal experience of religion was to be misunderstood and judged. The "people of the land" wanted to learn more about the Scripture but instead of being taught, they were excluded from the religious leaders' circle of friends. These leaders used their positions or quoted Scripture to drive people out of the "synagogue." These leaders actually drove out everyone who do not fit into their little boxes and agree with them. They taught the people to run away from their places of worship!

It's no surprise that the "sinners" were attracted to Jesus. He came to serve them instead of them serving Him. He treated them as fellow human beings. He valued each one as a person and not as an object to be judged and cast out. Jesus provided them a sense of worth instead of shame; He healed them instead of sending them away broken. Rather than exploiting them, He taught them that God loves everyone. He showed them direct access to God instead of going through rituals and tradition. He put people first over any systems or traditions.

I have a friend who was oppressed for many years under the authority of her pastor. She said that she suffered so much from it that she was "put on a shelf" for many years. She thought that they would value her and her service to the congregation. They became critical of her and stifled her talents and ability to minister with them. She did not measure up to their way of doing things and thought that she was competing against the church. Although she was fully committed and she submitted to authority, they thought that she was undermining the church for her own advantage. The church lost a valuable person and a good leader.

## Justice and mercy

*In the fourth year of King Darius, the word of the LORD came to Zechariah on the fourth day of the ninth month, the month of Kislev. The people of Bethel had sent Sharezer and Regem-Melek, together with their men, to entreat the LORD by asking the priests of the house of the LORD Almighty and the prophets, "Should I mourn and fast in the fifth month, as I have done for so many years?" Then the word of the LORD Almighty came to me: "Ask all the people of the land and the priests, 'When you fasted and mourned in the fifth and seventh months for the past seventy years, was it really for me that you fasted? And when you were eating and drinking, were you not just feasting for yourselves? Are these not the words the LORD proclaimed through the earlier prophets when Jerusalem and its surrounding towns were at rest and prosperous, and the Negev and the western foothills were settled?'" And the word of the LORD came again to Zechariah: "This is what the LORD Almighty said: 'Administer true justice; show mercy and compassion to one another. Do not oppress the widow or the fatherless, the foreigner or the poor. Do not plot evil against each other'"* (Zechariah 7:1-10).

Nebuchadnezzar, the king of Babylon, conquered Jerusalem in 597 BC deposing King Jehoiakim. Ten years later, he destroyed Jerusalem, including the Temple that King Solomon built. Nebuchadnezzar brought the people to captivity in Babylon. For 70 years during their captivity in Babylon, the people fasted regularly (verse 3, *Should I mourn and fast in the fifth month, as I have done for so many years?*) to remember the destruction of Jerusalem and the Temple. But since the Temple was being rebuilt, the people were wondering if they should continue to fast to remember the destruction of the Temple.

Customs and traditions do not carry the same authority
as the inspired Word of God.

Fasting became their tradition. Their intent was good, but their focus had deviated to the wrong direction as the Scripture said. Customs and traditions do not carry the same authority as the inspired Word of God.

## Justice instead of judgment

*Here is my servant whom I have chosen, the one I love, in whom I delight; I will put my Spirit on him, and he will proclaim justice to the nations* (Matthew 12:18).

The Pharisees accused Jesus that He came eating and drinking and they called Him glutton, drunkard and friend of sinners. What would our churches look like if the pews were filled with such people—friends of sinners? Would they be welcomed and greeted at the church doors or would they be judged once they got inside the church buildings? How would the church members react when they sit next to them—smelly, drunk and dirty?

One sunny day at one of the tiny towns in Indiana, I had a powerful encounter with God through our volunteers and a man who had become known as "the town lunatic"; we will call him Jim for the sake of privacy. We had come alongside the residents for a week of neighborhood makeover. There were many volunteers involved, both locals and from outside the town. One of our volunteers decided to go around town to meet with the residents. She was told by one of the town leaders to avoid a man that sits at the entrance of their town and not to talk to him. However, she came in contact with Jim and started to talk to him. I noticed she came back to our meeting place and asked one of our volunteers to come with her. Soon, about six people came with her to meet with Jim. It was the first time I saw this man. He was about 5'6", skinny with long unkempt hair and beard. His clothes were so dirty that they were covered with about a quarter inch of caked-on dust. You can only imagine his smell.

One of our volunteers, Bob, was a big man. As soon as Jim saw him, he asked him if he was a policeman. You could see from his face that he was very uncomfortable being in front of several people after many years of being unapproached and isolated. His speech was slurred and his voice was soft. We spoke to him and later introduced him to Jesus. He was somewhat reserved and hesitant. Toward the end of the conversation, the three women, Bob and I gave him hugs. His facial expression changed from being apprehensive to accepting. His eyes started to water and his countenance changed, and he accepted Jesus as his Lord.

Praying for the town outcast.

Several days after our weeklong outreach, my friend Bob visited him as he had promised Jim. Bob knocked on the door and spoke to Jim's mother. A clean-cut man came out of the room with a smile and shook Bob's hand. My friend could not believe his eyes—Jim was a different person! Transformed! He had cut his hair, trimmed his beard and took a shower. Later, he told Bob that he was going to the state fair with a friend. Jim was released from his captivity and he saw the goodness of God through the people who accepted him as he was. The tangible love of God transformed his perspective on life and his eternal future.

Jim was released from his captivity and he saw the goodness of God through the people who accepted him as he was.

## Mercy and compassion

*For I desire mercy, not sacrifice, and acknowledgment of God rather than burnt offerings* (Hosea 6:6).

God wants people to be treated equally and fairly. During Jesus' time, discrimination was common because of race, gender, religion and social status. One day, He was passing by Samaria on His way from Judea to Galilee. He could have taken other routes but He took the route less travelled by most Jews. There had been a long-standing animosity between the Jews and the Samaritans that they tried not to cross each other's paths. The Samaritans were a mixed race, part Jew and part Gentile, that grew out of the Assyrian captivity of the ten northern tribes in 727 BC. Rejected by the Jews because they could not prove their genealogy, the Samaritans established their own Temple and religious services on Mount Gerizim. Isn't this similar to our present day? Anyway, Jesus broke the tradition again when He spoke with a strange woman. A rabbi is not supposed to do that. Not only did He talk with her, He even asked her for a drink of water from a Samaritan well. One may read between the lines that He was up to something since they were by themselves.

Before she met Jesus, she was in a dark time of her life. She was in a valley; hopelessness, confusion and chaos seemed to follow her. That day, she had decided to draw water from a well. She chose to do it during the hottest part of the day because she wanted to avoid the people in her town who talked behind her back, to avoid being judged and ridiculed. She had quite a reputation in her own town. She had had five husbands and the man she was with currently was not even her husband. Regardless of the situation, she was a woman who could not keep a man. And this time, she was living with a man who was not her husband, probably to provide for her needs, or she may have been a prostitute making a living.

What do you think her emotional status was at that time of her life? No one liked her, she was a failure, people used her, abused her and dumped her afterward, and she was exploited. She most likely felt insecurity, fear, anxiety, remorse, shame, doubt and guilt.

We do not have to go far to meet people in similar situations who are in desperation like this woman. You can meet the homeless, the hungry and the thirsty all around us. We may call them the least, the lost and the last. Some of them may have lost their jobs and ended up in the streets. Some of them are drug addicts or alcoholics or even prostitutes. You will still meet people in the streets who are refugees from other cities and countries. Some of them just got divorced or were kicked out by their parents.

The depressed and the hopeless come clothed in different outward appearances. Some of them are wearing raggedy garments, pushing a cart with recyclable items and with all their belongings in it. Some of them are wearing nice clothes, suits and ties for men and nice dresses for women. Some of them have laptops, briefcases and own a nice car. They are executives, teachers, government officials and parents. Some of them are law enforcers and some hold prominent positions in our city.

Nonetheless, many of them are in a state of hopelessness or desperation. And they are looking for the answer, for hope and for the Truth. At one point in our life or another, there is a Samaritan woman inside each of us. Maybe you are in this kind of situation right now.

I was in a similar situation as the Samaritan woman. I was desperate, homeless, hopeless and looking for direction. I was confused and seeking answers in many different ways ... booze, drugs and women. Then Jesus came to give me Living Water. My life was changed. Jesus comes to you today offering you hope and unconditional love. Jesus is offering you today the Living Water. Take a drink and be refreshed and be washed clean by His blood. "Lord Jesus, forgive me from my sins. I repent and I receive you as my Lord and Savior. Thank you for dying on the cross for me. Come into my heart." I'd like to pause here to offer you our assistance in prayer. You can email us at merlin@fhlinternational.org if you want to know more about Jesus and change your eternal future.

He is looking for people who could be one of His
springs of water welling up to refresh and satisfy the thirsty.
Maybe you could be one.

Jesus answered her, *"If you knew the gift of God and who it is that asks you for a drink, you would have asked him and he would have given you living water, but whoever drinks the water I give him will never thirst. Indeed, the water I give him will become in him a spring of water welling up to eternal life"* (John 4:10, 14-15).

This is the kind of Kingdom that Jesus introduced and He is looking for people who will be conduits of eternal life to others through many practical ways. He is looking for people who could be one of His springs of water welling up to refresh and satisfy the thirsty. Maybe you could be one.

## The feeding of the 800

On July 25, 2009, I had the opportunity to witness God's unconditional love to humanity through the collaboration of more than 20 churches. Hundreds of hours of preparation paved the way to feed more than 800 people in downtown Indianapolis. The homeless were invited for lunch and for live Christian music. In addition, there were children's games, music, dance performance and lots of people serving the general public. People were fed physically and spiritually. One person accepted Christ as his Lord and Savior and changed his life for eternity. We had the privilege to hear his testimony. This is a simple way to reach out and to bring His tangible mercy to others.

The feeding was an outflow of God's grace to others. Compassion led many to see a miracle that day; in the blink of an eye, a person's life was changed for eternity.

Feeding of the 800 in downtown Indianapolis.

Feeding of the 800 brought 20 churches to work together.

The story of the Samaritan woman is not yet finished. Here's what happened: Many of the Samaritans from that town believed in him because of the woman's testimony, *"He told me everything I ever did."* So when the Samaritans came to him, they urged him to stay with them, and he stayed two days. And because of his words many more became believers. They said to the woman, *"We no longer believe just because of what you said; now we have heard for ourselves, and we know that this man really is the Savior of the world"* (John 4:39-42).

The Samaritan woman's story had a great ending. She was a not a Bible scholar nor had she been to any retreats or conferences. But she had a story to tell that could change people's lives. There are a lot of people out there waiting for you to tell your story. The Samaritan woman doesn't appear again in Scriptures, but the example of the woman at the well describes the spiritual thirst of the human heart for hope and Truth. No one can tell how many people were changed in her days and our days because of her testimony. What a great legacy and great story of redemption. Your legacy is still to be written; you just have to share your testimony and the goodness of God.

You and I are called to Royalty and Jesus is once again offering you a renewed life today. Whether you are in a hopeless situation or experiencing doubts, Jesus wants to heal you. He is waiting for you to have a renewed life, eternal life and hope.

## Let Your Kingdom come on earth

The Kingdom of God is already here on earth but not to its fullness until the "eschatological salvation." We live in between the First coming and the Second coming of Christ. However, Jesus did not compromise His teaching. He taught the unconditioned will of God upon human beings at all times and for all time. Our destiny depends upon our present decision. Our future is affected by our response and action today. We have a choice to make: we can decide to wait on the promises of God, putting off that which is available to receive presently, or we can choose to take hold of His promises now.

As Christians, we have been graced to receive what we don't deserve. The gifts are not based upon our works but upon our relationship with Him. Jesus commanded us to decide for our salvation, but gave us also the freedom to choose. When we decided to repent from our sin and accept Jesus as our Lord and Savior, in the blink of an eye we received His promised eternal life. We have actually been grafted or adopted into the family of God and we receive the same Spirit that raised Jesus from the dead. The Spirit lives in us forever and will be our Advocate in any life situation. He works through us and He provides us all the resources from heaven and earth to make sure that we fulfill what we were called to do—no matter what it is.

I would rank being saved as the most powerful miracle that we can ever have in this world. From the kingdom of darkness to the Kingdom of the Light—a person's life is changed eternally! That is beyond seeing people healed immediately, people being released from demonic oppression, and seeing the dead raised back to life—although those things are pretty amazing too! When He said to preach the Gospel, heal the sick, and to cast out demons... He meant it (Mark 16:15-18). You can read books about people who came back to life to tell their story after they had experienced physical death in their bodies, stories of miraculous healings and prophecies.

It is up to us to decide whether we want to be used supernaturally by Him or not. We can decide to leave it to others, the ones who may be branded as "weird" and those who "do things through the power of the devil." Why is it that, for most people, it is easier to believe a person who is demon-possessed is capable of doing supernatural things while the people of God are less capable of doing such things? Are some of our leaders actually preventing their people from seeing miracles or to be miracle workers? Why is it easier to doubt than to trust that we have the Holy Spirit as our Advocate? Do most people give the devil more power than God over their lives? Is that kind of thinking demonic or idolatry—giving more importance to darkness over the God who is above all things? Idolatry means "excessive or blind adoration, reverence, devotion" (Dictionary. com). I heard from a friend of mine that one of the reasons why some of the young generations resort to witchcraft is because they do not see the supernatural in our churches. They just hear and read about it but they do not experience the power of God in their lives. We owe it to the next generation. We produce who we are.

There are a lot of people out there
waiting for you to tell your story.

———

*Then they brought him a demon-possessed man who was blind and mute, and Jesus healed him, so that he could both talk and see. All the people were astonished and said, "Could this be the Son of David?" But when the Pharisees heard this, they said, "It is only by Beelzebul, the prince of demons, that this fellow drives out demons"* (Matthew 12:22-24).

Jesus did a miracle and He was accused of operating under the power of satan. Then Jesus said in verse 30, "*Whoever is not with me is against me, and whoever does not gather with me scatters.*" Where do you stand? Choose wisely; decide for yourself. Jesus may ask you the same question today.

Here's what the Bible says: The prince of this earth is satan. He's the deceiver and the accuser; he has the power to give the kingdom of the world (Luke 4:5-6). He can enter into a person, he can afflict people, he masquerades as an angel of light, and he has a synagogue (Rev. 2:9). However, we know that Jesus is the King of all Kings, we have the Advocate who never leaves us, and we are given authority over satan and his demons, in the authority of the name of Jesus. We are given authority over the works of the devil and we were commanded to be the light of the world. The word "authority" indicates the right to use power. We have the delegated power from the King of Kings to operate in the power of the Holy Spirit.

Next, we will look at some of the works of Jesus in demonstrating the Kingdom of God and some present-day testimonies.

## The Kingdom can be realized now

Jesus was called many negative names, like blasphemer and friend of sinners. They said he drives out demons by the prince of demons; even his own relatives did not believe him.

Jesus said to them, *"A prophet is not without honor except in his own town, among his relatives and in his own home." He could not do any miracles there, except lay his hands on a few sick people and heal them. He was amazed at their lack of faith"* (Mark 6:4-6). Verse 5 is one of the verses that is most challenging: *He could not do any miracles there, except lay his hands on a few sick people and heal them.* Jesus, the incarnate God, was not able to do "any miracles" in His own town because of the people's lack of faith. Because of the people's response of unbelief, they missed the Kingdom spreading in their town. If people are unwilling to receive, then they rob themselves of the gifts, in this case, miracles.

On the other hand, in Matthew 15:21-28, Jesus was stopped by a Canaanite woman asking Him to heal her suffering daughter who was demon-possessed. In this story, it seemed like Jesus challenged the faith of the mother. Even the disciples urged Him to send the woman away because she kept crying out after them. However, the mother persisted even more by kneeling down in front of Jesus. Even then, Jesus seemed not willing to help her. In spite of it, the mother continued in her perseverance. Then Jesus said (verse 28), *"Woman, you have great faith! Your request is granted."* Her daughter was healed at that moment.Could it be that many of us miss the blessings because of our faith? Would our unbelief hinder Jesus from doing miracles (Mark 6:5)? In certain instances, we miss the miracle because we refuse to receive and believe that miracles still happen. In fact, you could be the miracle that others have been waiting for.

While I was still volunteering at a hospital, I visited a man in his 60s. His face reflected the excruciating pain in his knee. He was blaming the nurse for giving his pain medicine too late. I asked if I could pray for him. He gladly and thankfully said yes. I put my hand on his knee and asked the Lord to heal him. Immediately, I saw his face change its appearance from excruciating to peaceful. He then said, "I can feel it now."

I said, "Good, the pain medicine finally took effect."

I almost fell down when he said in a normal voice, "No, not the medicine, but your prayer!" I did not know what to say; I just smiled and left the room. Those words stayed with me the rest of the day. He had great faith and was willing to receive; his request was granted. He received the miracle!

## Release the captives

*When Jesus stepped ashore, he was met by a demon-possessed man from the town. For a long time this man had not worn clothes or lived in a house, but had lived in the tombs. When he saw Jesus, he cried out and fell at his feet, shouting at the top of his voice, "What do you want with me, Jesus, Son of the Most High God? I beg you, don't torture me!" For Jesus had commanded the impure spirit to come out of the man. Many times it had seized him, and though he was chained hand and foot and kept under guard, he had broken his chains and had been driven by the demon into solitary places* (Luke 8:27-29).

Many times, we read in Scriptures that Jesus frequented places where most people would not go. The devil can do so much damage to a person. As was the case with this demon-oppressed man in Scripture, he can torture by robbing you of sanity, causing you to hurt yourself and be isolated away from families and friends, and living in strange places to survive. This story reveals that satan can afflict people for years in our society. They end up in institutions and never get healing or help. Jesus still heals people and He still does miracles.

About three years ago, I was attending a Christian conference on the north side of Indianapolis. For some reason I felt I should sit in a particular area away from my friends. In the middle of the conference, I heard strange sounds coming from the lady behind me. I tried to disregard it but the noise got weirder and louder. In order not to disrupt the conference, I silently escorted the person outside of the crowd with her friend. She started to twitch, her body got stiff and her eyes changed! I knew that demons were manifesting and trying to interrupt the conference and to divert the attention of the attendees.

After making our way out of the sanctuary, we sat her on a chair. She started to cough heavily and threw up while her body became rigid and jerky. She faced us and made clawing gestures with her hands while taunting us. She would cry with agony and then suddenly she would laugh. Her eyes changed their appearance as if she would attack us followed by the clawing gestures. Another friend of mine came and she confronted the demon to leave and not manifest anymore. After a few minutes, the demons left. We found out from the person that she had sins that opened the door to the demons to get into her. Starting that night, we became friends. Currently, she volunteers regularly for our ministry and she also co-leads a Bible study group with her pastor.

Jesus still heals people and He still does miracles.

## Glory in our midst

*Jesus said to the servants, "Fill the jars with water," so they filled them to the brim. Then he told them, "Now draw some out and take it to the master of the banquet" (John 2:7-8).*

The Scripture recorded that the first miracle of Jesus was turning water into wine. Imagine if you were one of His disciples who brought a jar of water to the master of the ceremonies knowing that the jar was just filled with water. Jesus reveals His glory by involving the disciples in the miracle-making. Somehow, the water was turned into wine sometime after it was poured into the jar and before the master of ceremonies drank it. This miracle was similar to the feeding of the 5,000. The bread and the fish multiplied as the disciples distributed them to those in need.

In the summer of 2011, my wife Annie, Bill (one of our ministry directors) and I went to a Christian conference in Ohio. There were hundreds of people in this conference. At the end of the first session, they offered prayers to everyone before they went to break and in preparation for the next session. There were several people positioned to pray for others, and one of them was this bald man whose head and face were completely glittering with gold dust! I was intrigued and lined up so he could pray for me. I took a picture of him and his sparkly head while he was praying for my friend Bill. The following day, he and his wife were introduced to the audience. His wife told us the story of how her husband's gold-dusted head came to be... She and her daughter were out of town and he was missing her terribly. He was crying out to the Lord and the Lord told him to worship Him. One day, he was praying and waiting for God's glory. After days of intense prayer, he noticed his dogs began barking and he saw gold dust on himself. Since then, even after he showers, the gold dust keeps reappearing on his head! He had prayed for the glory of God and it now rested on him, manifested in gold dust all over his head. This is a phenomenon that may not be able to be explained by our minds. The supernatural invaded the natural. God is using this person to reveal His glory similar to what Jesus did with His disciples. He wants us to be miracle-workers and to be carriers of His Glory.

The miracles strengthened the disciples' faith in Jesus. They were a sign of Jesus' glory but not the only evidence that proved He's the Son of God. We do not worship signs, wonders and miracles but we worship the source of them, the person—Jesus, the Son of God.

*Is not this the kind of fasting I have chosen: to loose the chains of injustice and untie the cords of the yoke, to set the oppressed free and break every yoke? Is it not to share your food with the hungry and to provide the poor wanderer with shelter—when you see the naked, to clothe them, and not to turn away from your own flesh and blood? Then your light will break forth like the dawn, and your healing will quickly appear; then your righteousness will go before you, and the glory of the LORD will be your rear guard. Then you will call, and the LORD will answer; you will cry for help, and he will say: Here am I (Isaiah 58:6-9).*

We do not worship signs, wonders and miracles
but we worship the source of them,
the person—Jesus, the Son of God.

———

Jesus inaugurated the Kingdom. When we received Him as our Savior, we were adopted into His family. He modeled the ways of the Kingdom so we can follow His examples. We are called to be His representatives and His ambassadors to the earth. We have the Spirit of God within us, which means that we become the carriers of His presence. We become the vehicles and the living testimonies of the Age to come.

In the next part of this book, we will explore the exciting possibilities that God had called us to.

## QUESTIONS FOR STUDY

1. When you look at your city, can you say that God is present there? Why? Have you experienced or witnessed a miracle? Describe what happened.

_____

_____

_____

_____

2. In Acts 3:6, Peter commanded the healing to come to the lame man in the name of Jesus instead of praying to God to heal him. Did the name of Jesus heal the man? Why? Read Matthew 7:21-23. Why do you think Jesus said it?

_____

_____

_____

_____

3. In Matthew 23:1-3, Jesus was blunt with the teachers of the law and Pharisees. Do you think His statement is still true today? Explain and give examples. How would you address your leader if he/she was guilty of the same?

_____

_____

_____

_____

4. Jesus likes to answer a question with a question. Why? Read Matthew 15:1-3. Are you holding onto any traditions that have now become stumbling blocks for their purpose? Read Matthew 15:1-3.

_____

_____

_____

_____

5. Why do you think Jesus had more conflicts with the teachers of the law and Pharisees than with the sinners? Is this still true today? Why?

_____

_____

_____

_____

6. Jesus came to earth to offer hope and eternal life to anyone who will put their faith in Him and accept Him as Lord over his/her life. If you do not have a personal relationship with Jesus, ask your pastor or someone in your group to help you to know Jesus.

_____

_____

_____

_____


7. Why do you think that, for most people, it is easier to believe a person who is demon-possessed is capable of doing supernatural things while the people of God are less capable of doing such things? Read Mark 3:20-22. Why do you think the "experts" of Jesus' time had a hard time believing in Him?

_____

_____

_____

_____

8. Would our unbelief hinder Jesus from doing miracles (Mark 6:1-6)?

_____

_____

_____

_____

9. Read John 2:1-9. Jesus told the servants to fill the jars with water. He did not ask them to change the water into wine. Have you ever had an experience in your life when you felt God wanted you to do something and you didn't know why, and through your obedience, He did a miraculous thing? Yes or no. Describe the situation. What happened after you obeyed or disobeyed Him?

_____

_____

_____

_____

10. Action Step: Ask God to provide you an opportunity in the next 2 weeks to introduce Jesus to someone in your family, school, workplace or neighborhood.

_____

_____

_____

_____

11. Action Step: In the next 2 weeks, ask God to open your eyes to step out in faith to do something out of the ordinary, such as praying for people in the streets, praying for the sick, visiting a nursing home or hospital, or something radical such as going to city hall to pray for the mayor and his/her staff, worshiping God in public places such as street corners, living out your faith in your workplace and marketplace.

_____

_____

_____

_____

# PART THREE

The Kingdom

In Our Midst

Once, on being asked by the Pharisees when the kingdom of God would come, Jesus replied, "The coming of the kingdom of God is not something that can be observed, nor will people say, 'Here it is,' or 'There it is,' because the kingdom of God is in your midst.

—LUKE 17:20-21

Is the Kingdom in our midst a myth, a mystery or a reality in your life? At the beginning of this book, we read some of the answers to the question, "What would your neighborhood look like if you could say, 'The Kingdom of God is here.'?" This question gets people thinking of the possibilities through God's presence in their communities. Change happens when we become aware of our current situation. We have to be careful not to become accustomed to the world's norm for we are not citizens of this world (Phil 3:20). The danger is that we may just settle for the status quo or not do anything to improve our current situation.

*"See, I have given you this land. Go in and take possession of the land the LORD swore he would give to your fathers—to Abraham, Isaac and Jacob—and to their descendants after them"* (Deut 1:8). God has given us our neighborhoods for Christ, but we have to "go in and occupy it." After we "take the land," we need to share the Gospel and influence the inhabitants with the Kingdom of God.

## Moving forward with God against all odds

Through partnering with local organizations and residents, we can find the needs. Once we find out the needs, we encourage the residents to develop their own projects. After they conceptualize and develop their projects, we guide them to identify the resources needed to complete the projects. They are trained how to recruit volunteers and how to engage the community toward common good. These all seem simple, but I have seen it many times that pastors of community churches within a mile radius of each other sometimes do not know each other, let alone work together. Because of the busyness in the ministry, it's hard to get to know others in the land.

On the other hand, there are a few neighborhoods and leaders that get stuck in finding out every possible detail where the resources would come from before they ever identify and develop the projects. They worry about the things they may not need anyway. But this is the way of our society. The world teaches us to develop budget first and base our plans out of what we have available, and then we can decide what to do. The Kingdom of God says the opposite: *Seek the Kingdom of God and its righteousness first and all of these will be added unto you.*

*The Lord now chose seventy-two other disciples and sent them ahead in pairs to all the towns and places he planned to visit. These were his instructions to them: "The harvest is great, but the workers are few. So pray to the Lord who is in charge of the harvest; ask him to send more workers into his fields. Now go, and remember that I am sending you out as lambs among wolves. Don't take any money with you, nor a traveler's bag, nor an extra pair of sandals* (Luke 10:1-4). Instead of asking His disciples to come up with money and resources to bring with them, Jesus told them the opposite. He told them not to bring anything and not to bother bringing stuff they may not need anyway. He wanted them to rely on Him for whatever they need since it was His idea to send them. When God tells us to do something, He will surely provide everything we needed to accomplish the task...His way.

This is a hard faith concept to live out—it's one of those things that sounds very good when you're preaching it, but difficult to do. What would the church elders say if there's not enough money in the bank at the end of the month? The non-profit board members would confront the founder or the executive director if they didn't have a budget, and yet the organization is going public to do lots of community services. Where do you draw the line when your financial statement won't allow you to move and do the things you sense are the Lord's will? Planning is good, but leaving room for God's hand to be in it is the absolute best.

We are all guilty at one time or another of changing God's plan because we think ours is better than His! Sometimes we add or take out something so we can help God by modifying His plan because we think things would work out better.

God had reminded the Israelites of the Promised Land flowing with milk and honey. The twelve explorers surveyed the land for 40 days and indeed, they found out the land was fertile and very suitable to raise their families. But they also found out there were giants in the land. Ten out of twelve said that the inhabitants would annihilate them. They spread bad news to the rest of the Israelites that the inhabitants were stronger and more powerful than they. Even though God had promised them complete victory and commanded them to "take the land," they were overwhelmed by their analytical minds and decided the "giants" of the land were more powerful than the God who promised them the land. They trusted their eyes more than God. So they came up with their own plan...go back to slavery in

Egypt. Caleb and Joshua saw the giants as well, but they believed God at His word and were ready to take the land. They wouldn't settle for less, unlike the 10 who felt defeated even before the battle started. Instead, they saw a place of opportunity perfect to raise their families and the future crops that would come from the fertile land. They saw the giants as having no protection. They saw that the giants would be helpless prey to them because God was not with them.

In my years of working with different churches, I have seen history repeat itself. So many of them were hesitant to occupy the land—their neighborhoods—because they saw the "giants" of the land: opposition in the form of limited resources, drug dealers and criminals, or even other churches and ministries that would discourage them, and inhabitants who would refuse to buy into what they had to say and do. Thus, many of our dark neighborhoods remain dark and have even become darker; instead of bringing the Light of God, the darkness continues to creep in because we have allowed it. That's the opposite of what God wants in our communities.

Our neighborhoods are waiting for Christians who will take the land back from the drug dealers, prostitutes, corruption, gangs and from demonic oppression. These "giants" of the land must be taken down by those who will take God at His word. Christians have the delegated authority from God and a mandate to conquer the land. Jesus has given us the Holy Spirit, our Advocate, to operate in the heavenly dimension and to invade our neighborhoods with the power of God.

The promise has been decreed, proclaimed and spoken; it's ours for the taking! The opportunity to transform the land and to bring the light is inevitable. Turning the opportunity to reality is our next topic.

## Stepping into action

We have to take action to receive the promise. Taking possession means work. Unfortunately, when we hear the word "work" many of us back away because of the busyness and priorities of our own lives. We're bombarded with multiple distractions and enamored with the conveniences of modern living that, in contrast, make our lives complicated.

In order for us to take action, we have to be fully convinced of the promise and have faith in the Promise-giver. We are motivated by our thoughts and our emotion before we take action. If our minds and hearts fully believe His promises, nothing can stop us toward possessing the land. However, if we just know the promise, but our hearts do not receive it, we will have internal civil war; thus Jesus said that a kingdom divided would not stand. When the "waves" of challenges come, we will not be motivated to action; instead we will do more complaining and will convince others it cannot be done—similar to the 10 spies.

Jesus has something to say about this in Matthew 15:14: *"Leave them; they are blind guides. If the blind lead the blind, both will fall into a pit."* We have to be careful not to be influenced by others who have good intention; good intention alone is not enough to follow them.

Later in the story, the 10 spies spread the bad report among the Israelites. They had good intentions, but wrong motives. The majority of the people believed them. Not only did they begin to weep, but also they protested against Moses and Aaron. They degraded themselves for settling for less than what they were destined to. They reasoned that it would be better for them to die in Egypt as slaves rather than taking the "promised" land. They did not want to risk their perceived security and venture into the new land. Scripture says they rebelled against God by not taking action and treated God with contempt. They justified themselves and convinced others to believe them.

Our society needs to take back what was lost at the Garden of Eden: our dominion over His creation. When Eve and Adam sinned, humanity lost its kingship; sin and death reigned over the earth (Rom 5:12). As Christians, we are commanded to "take and possess the land." When Jesus left the earth, He commissioned us to heal the sick, feed the hungry and release those in bondage. We are to push back the darkness and to spread the light wherever we go. We become the light of the world. So how do we shine our light right now in our neighborhoods?

## Awareness

Let's look even deeper into awareness. If we become more mindful of God's presence in our midst, we will focus our lives on God's promises rather than the customs and behaviors of this world. We have to change our perception of God and our reaction to the world. Paul said, "*Do not conform to the pattern of this world, but be transformed by the renewing of your mind.*

*Then you will be able to test and approve what God's will is — his good, pleasing and perfect will"* (Rom 12:2a). Our actions come from our decisions and our decisions come from our experience, thinking and emotions. If the things of heaven dominate our minds, we will act and behave more as children of God. This means that our consciousness should be focused on the things of the Kingdom rather than the way of the world. As Paul said, we are to imitate Christ, influencing the world with the promises of God through His Spirit in us.

The world says that we have to follow their system in order to succeed in life. However, Scripture says *"For the wisdom of this world is foolishness in God's sight"* (1 Cor. 3:19).

Just 10 years ago, who would have thought that many of our young men would wear pants so low that most of their underwear would hang out? Or that they would have to walk with their legs far apart to prevent their pants from falling down and use one hand on their crotch to keep pulling them up? They call it fashion! More and more people are accepting it as the "new norm" because we see it everywhere. Our minds become accustomed to it and slowly we do not become aware of the obvious. We eventually accept it as normal and the worst thing is that our society is influenced and our generations submit to the schemes of the devil.

Another obvious example that is subtly infiltrating our homes are the TV shows that are entertaining and bringing families together but whose contents are inappropriate for young viewers. One will notice that the most popular shows promote sex, violence and greed. Apostle Paul reminded us of this in Romans 1:29-30, *"They have become filled with every kind of wickedness, evil, greed and depravity. They are full of envy, murder, strife, deceit and malice. They are gossips, slanderers, God-haters, insolent, arrogant and boastful; they invent ways of doing evil; they disobey their parents; they have no understanding, no fidelity, no love, no mercy."* Paul knows the dangers of tolerating the cunning schemes of satan, who is using the strategy that sends many people in a downward spiral. Apathy slowly seeps in, and when apathy matures, we disengage and become hopeless that things will ever change. This process will pull us down into the pit of despair—the very thing the devil wants. He wants us to change our state of mind and to believe things are not going to change. We become convinced it is impossible to go against the world, such as the case of the majority of the Israelites during Moses' time. The world won over their destiny. We all can fall victim to this if we are not aware of the subtlety of this trick.

On the other hand, once the things of heaven saturate us and we receive in our minds the promises of God, we start moving in new directions. What would happen around us if our mindsets are on heavenly things and not on earthly things? Even though the world says it cannot be done, or the majority of the people just wish it will happen in future, we can take action now to see the promise become a reality in our lifetime. We don't wait for the economy to change; we change the economy. We don't watch to see what will happen to our neighborhoods; we take action to change the course of history. The impossible becomes possible and the miracles become regular occurrences in our daily lives.

We shatter the tradition and we challenge the normal ways of our surroundings. We pursue the promise until it becomes a reality. We influence our society instead of being conformed to the way of the world. Once our focus permeates our entire being, we start to access the sphere of heaven until we take hold of the promise. We were created in the image of God and God had deposited His Spirit in us.

We don't watch to see what will happen to our neighborhoods; we take action to change the course of history.

So, how's your image of yourself? Better yet, how's your image of God? Our cities are waiting to be transformed by our actions powered by the Holy Spirit. The world is watching us to see if our words and beliefs are backed by our action.

Satan and his demons are having a heyday with us when we think defeating thoughts because he knows he can instill in us the first thought he used against Adam and Eve—doubt. Doubt when given power over our lives, can be a poison that contaminates our entire being. It manifests in our minds, affecting our entire physical being until it has direct impact in our spiritual lives.

Doubt immobilizes us even when we know the promise is ours for the taking. Doubt is a negative power that prevents us from taking the right action. We need to have a counter-strategy against doubt.

In order for things to change, we have to take actions. As the apostle James said, faith without action is dead. Our actions are a product of our being, which includes our faith, abilities and determination. I have seen neighborhoods with an aggregate consciousness of poverty and helplessness. You can feel it in the air and you can see it in the attitude of the residents. As the Bible says, all creation is groaning. But the collective consciousness of our neighborhoods can change the spiritual atmosphere of a region; our thoughts can affect what is unseen in the supernatural. So, if more people become aware of the presence of God in their city, they will do things that reflect the rule of God. They will actually "break the rule" imposed on them by the world.

It is generally true that the entire neighborhood will experience the effects of the mentality and actions of the majority, whether good or bad. We manifest what we first conceive in our minds, and our physical body follows what our minds tell us. *For as he thinks in his heart, so is he* (Proverb 23:7, NKJV). In the case of negative thinking patterns, our minds can be reverse-trained to learn new habits. This new habit can revolutionize a person and can transform neighborhoods. Expressing the love of God is contagious and can radically move the inhabitants toward a new way of living.

The impossibilities that were ingrained in our mind by tradition and customs should be questioned. We need to set our mental and spiritual attitude to affect our actions. This intentional mindfulness will make ways to the supernatural power of God in our neighborhoods. We have to be convinced that the Holy Spirit actually lives in us; He wants us to transform our neighborhoods as Jesus did. Jesus is our model; He only did what the Father does and He only spoke what the Father speaks. That's the model of being aware of what God wants in our cities.

how's your image of yourself? Better yet, how's your image of God? Our cities are waiting to be transformed by our actions powered by the Holy Spirit.

To wake people up from their slumber, Jesus said in Matthew 5:13, *"You are the salt of the earth. But what good is salt if it has lost its flavor?"* If we are followers of Christ, then we should follow His teachings and do what He modeled for us. Otherwise, we just think, but do not act. Let's not deceive ourselves. James 1:22-24 says, *Anyone who listens to the word, but does not do what it says is like someone who looks at his face in a mirror and, after looking at himself, goes away and immediately forgets what he looks like.*

## Kingdom reality

*Jesus returned to Galilee in the power of the Spirit, and news about him spread through the whole countryside. He taught in their synagogues, and everyone praised him.*

*He went to Nazareth, where he had been brought up, and on the Sabbath day he went into the synagogue, as was his custom. And he stood up to read. The scroll of the prophet Isaiah was handed to him. Unrolling it, he found the place where it is written:*

"The Spirit of the Lord is on me, because he has anointed me to preach good news to the poor. He has sent me to proclaim freedom for the prisoners and recovery of sight for the blind, to release the oppressed, to proclaim the year of the Lord's favor."

*Then he rolled up the scroll, gave it back to the attendant and sat down. The eyes of everyone in the synagogue were fastened on him, and he began by saying to them, "Today this scripture is fulfilled in your hearing"* (Luke 4:14-21).

Jesus revealed the Kingdom reality—His creation assumes its proper position. He took the authority given to Him and demonstrated the Kingdom culture here on earth. It was foreign to everyone, especially to the religious people of the day. He brought Heaven's perspective to a world that was created to be a reflection of the Kingdom, which had drifted away from its original form.

What does this mean for us NOW? As Christians, we follow Jesus' model on how to operate and how to live out the Kingdom. The time of salvation has begun…*"Today this scripture is fulfilled in your hearing."*

## Preach the Good News to the poor

The word "preach" was intended to evangelize—not only to deliver the Word to the ears of the listeners, but also to reach the heart, to influence people according to the Scripture. What is the Good News? Jesus died on the cross to defeat sin and death. He rose up again. He who turns away from his sin and receives Jesus as his Savior will receive eternal life.

It is still the same Good News that we preach, although it may be a little different approach than 100 years ago or 50 years ago. We have to be innovative and explore the land once again. For example, the Internet and social media are new tools to reach the world right in our city. We may still walk the streets and knock on doors to share the Gospel, however we can also use acts of kindness to reach out to those who may not listen to us otherwise. It is not about our fluent speech, but what God can do through us when we go out and allow God to use us. Preaching the Good News involves more than just words, it also involves action motivated by our hearts. Our hearts need to be circumcised and transformed by allowing the Holy Spirit to permeate it with His presence.

This year (2012), one of our groups decided to offer a basketball tournament to their community as a way to bring the love of God to the youth through a sporting event. The group started the day by sharing testimonies of how God changed their lives. Sharing the Gospel followed these testimonies, then they played basketball. After three days, more than 50 youth accepted Jesus and rededicated their lives to God.

Sharing of the Gospel at a basketball outreach.

Praying for the kids at a basketball outreach.

The Kingdom of God is at hand...Preach the Good News to the poor.

## Proclaim freedom for the prisoners

Proclaiming freedom for the prisoners means more than just those who are incarcerated in jail—it can mean any kind of bondage. Many of us live under different kinds of captivity. It is our job to introduce prisoners to Christ and to be conduits of the freedom He is offering them.

In 2010, our staff met refugees from other countries. Their own people persecuted them and they had no choice except to leave their own country. Many of them had experienced living in a few refugee camps in other countries before coming to the U.S. They were mistreated and cast out of their own countries. So by the time they reached the U.S., they had been humiliated many times and many of them had lost their self-worth and identity.

Merlin helping refugee at food pantry.

Nepali home church in the Word.

Nepali home church grows.

We were introduced to them through our food pantry and other outreaches. During a Christmas outreach, the young refugees came to us asking if we would start church services in one of their apartments. We agreed to do it with the understanding that they become self-sufficient in the future. Our ministry gave them Bibles, guitars and guitar lessons, and life skills training such as dental classes. We got to know them well, and we ate and worshipped together. After a few weeks of our services, many people accepted Christ on one particular day. That same day, I was prompted by the Holy Spirit to ask them if they want to be baptized. By the end of the service, I baptized 24 refugees in an apartment bathtub. They were released from their captivity through the power of the Gospel.

Nepali home church teaching dental hygiene.

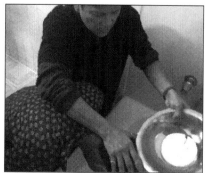
Nepali home church performing baptism in an apartment bathtub.

Many people were baptized at the end of the service.

We could be prisoners of sickness and disease through the affliction of the spirit of darkness.

*They went to Capernaum, and when the Sabbath came, Jesus went into the synagogue and began to teach. The people were amazed at his teaching, because he taught them as one who had authority, not as the teachers of the law. Just then a man in their synagogue who was possessed by an impure spirit cried out, "What do you want with us, Jesus of Nazareth? Have you come to destroy us? I know who you are—the Holy One of God!"*

*"Be quiet!" said Jesus sternly. "Come out of him!" The impure spirit shook the man violently and came out of him with a shriek* (Mark 1:21-26).

Jesus presented the Gospel in its wholeness. Whenever He taught about the Kingdom of God, He would heal people. John Wimber, founder of the Vineyard Movement, stated in his book *Power Evangelism,* that out of 3,774 verses in the four Gospels, 484 (12 percent of the total) relate specifically to the healing of physical and mental illness and the resurrection of the dead. Jesus spent more time healing and casting out demons than preaching. That's why He said in Matthew 10:7-8 (NASB), *"And as you go, preach, saying, 'The kingdom of heaven is at hand.' Heal the sick, raise the dead, cleanse the lepers, cast out demons. Freely you received, freely give."*

The Kingdom of God is at hand...Proclaim freedom for the prisoners.

Merlin playing basketball with a boy who had an eye problem.

Oil change for single moms.

## Recovery of sight for the blind

A few years ago, our team did a free oil change outreach for abused and single mothers in our community. While the oil change was being performed for the mothers, we had a team praying for the mothers and their children. I was able to play basketball with one of the boys. After a few minutes of trying to make a goal, suddenly I was prompted by the Holy Spirit to pray for him. He was not resistant, but he was a little apprehensive when I asked him if I could pray for him. My next move actually startled him... I felt led by the Holy Spirit to ask him if I could put spit on his right eye. He agreed and I prayed for him. His mother saw me praying for him and afterward, she told me that he had bad eyesight on the eye I had put spit on. She told me that he saw some horrible things done by his father and, consequently, it had impacted him physically. After I prayed for him, his eyesight got better and he was astounded by what had happened. I prayed that as he was healed physically, his heart would see the goodness of God in spite of what had happened in the past.

*They arrived at Bethsaida. Some people brought a sightless man and begged Jesus to give him a healing touch. Taking him by the hand, he led him out of the village. He put spit in the man's eyes, laid hands on him, and asked, "Do you see anything?"*

*He looked up. "I see men. They look like walking trees." So Jesus laid hands on his eyes again. The man looked hard and realized that he had recovered perfect sight, saw everything in bright, twenty-twenty focus* (Mark 8:22-26, The Message).

The Kingdom of God is at hand...Recovery of sight for the blind. Release the oppressed.

## The Lord's favor

"The Lord's favor." The Gospel of Christ is preached and being preached to the present age—this is a favor granted to us. One of the innovative evangelism techniques we thought of was for our women to visit go-go dancer clubs in Indianapolis. There is one area in Indianapolis where several of these clubs are located. I spoke with many people who have a heart for the oppressed women to release the Lord's power in these dark places. Because of the possible dangers of this kind of outreach, we spent several days of careful planning before they went into these establishments. As safeguards, we sent several men along with them to stay outside of the clubs for protection, and we had prayer teams who prayed for them continually that evening. To get the women into the clubs, I thought of offering the dancers free oil changes. We had our team tell the bouncers and the managers that we were giving away free oil changes to the single moms. It made sense for them since most of the dancers are single mothers. However, even with a good plan, our team met some opposition to get in. But somehow God made a way for them to go into the clubs. When you are operating in the Kingdom, you gain favor with God and men... "And Jesus grew in wisdom and stature, and in favor with God and men" (Luke 2:52).

Inside the club, our team saw the women dancing for the customers. They were able to speak with and pray for a few dancers after their "dance" time. By the end of the night, they were able to visit a few clubs and had prayed for several women. One of our volunteers, Jane, was about to pray for one of the dancers, but she was told that she was up next to dance. She told Jane not to go away, that she'd be back after her dance. She returned right away! The Lord had caused the circumstance to change for this precious daughter of His so that she could be ministered to. Someone else took her place and she returned to ask Jane to pray for her. Not only did this make an impact on the dancer's life, it touched our volunteer deep in her heart how the Lord used her that day. Our team took the Gospel into the dark places. They were able to share the love of Christ with them. *For I will give you words and wisdom that none of your adversaries will be able to resist or contradict* (Luke 21:15). Living a lifestyle of unconditional love allows us to live in freedom and bring the Kingdom of God into the hearts of others!

The Kingdom of God is at hand...The Lord's favor.

## A new perspective

March 17-23, 2002 was the week my life was transformed and launched a ministry that is now reaching the churches, businesses, government and other sectors of our society. I was encouraged by my friend, Tim, to go for the first time on a short-term mission trip to Costa Rica. Our team would be constructing a church building in a community on top of a mountain with no running water or electricity. We would be ministering to the Bri-Bri Indians and we would be putting our tents in a clearing since the only building available to sleep in was the old church building with lots of windows and thousands of mosquitoes.

I wasn't sure if I would be able to join the group since I didn't have enough money to go. But as it turned out I was able to take vacation and raised enough money to join the team. The idea of tenting in a wilderness surrounded by mountain ranges and to interact with the natives gave me a sense of adventure. I felt it would give me a chance to help in construction and also practice my evangelism techniques. I thought that I could provide the natives spiritual answers that could change their lives.

It was an adventure to travel to a mountain with no running water and electricity. The pastor met us when we got to our final destination and we started the construction right away. It was hot and humid during the day, but cool during the evening. I will always cherish the memories of that trip—nights alone in my tent looking up at the starry sky while listening to the fascinating sounds of insects and the wild, or the morning when I was awakened by a loud scream from one of the missionaries as she was about to go into the outhouse and discovered a large snake on the roof.

Costa Rica muddy road back to town.

Merlin working in Costa Rica.

Inside a Costa Rican Bri-Bri home.

Many of the missionaries, including me, slept in tents near the old church (Costa Rica).

Volunteers raising a church roof in Costa Rica.

Almost every day it rained hard, making the clay road up and down the mountain very treacherous to navigate. However, it was refreshing to have rain in a hot and humid place. On our third night, we invited the community for a night of worship. The attendees came walking up the dark, unpaved road; some had walked for two hours just to join us that night. The worship was great and it seemed like it went for a few hours. We were able to pray for everyone. I started to develop friendships with my fellow missionaries and the natives. Somehow, I gained the trust of the natives and their children. It was great to interact and play with the children.

As the days went by, we had accomplished very little construction and I was feeling like we hadn't really done what we came to do. Then, our last night turned out to be very special. I felt like the Holy Spirit visited us as we prayed for people. Most of them were weeping and were sweating bullets during the prayer time. It was very special to me to see how the natives worshiped the Lord with reckless abandon. One of the natives who assisted in the construction and whom I befriended accepted the Lord in his heart.

Saying good-bye was very hard and I promised the pastor I would be back. When I returned to the states I was a changed man. It seemed like God had provided me new sets of ears and eyes. The things that were important to me in the past had lost their significance and were replaced by a new zest for my life. My perspectives changed and my priorities were rearranged. My heart was altered and my mind was renewed. I started to hunger for God and wanted to go back to the mission field right away.

I was very excited when my church planned a second trip there. However, I was not able to go with them because I couldn't afford it moneywise or timewise. I was very disappointed; I waited until the next trip, but the same thing happened.

## Mission trip in your own backyard

After more than two years of trying and failing to go back to the mission field, I had the thought that there must be many people like me who have the heart to go on a mission, but who don't have the time or money to go. I thought, why not do something similar to taking people outside the country?— Why not have a mission week in our own neighborhoods that would be available to many community churches in the area? The verses in Acts 1:8 made sense to me that we should reach out first to our own Jerusalem, then to Judea, Samaria and to the ends of the earth.

In February 2005, I contacted 35 pastors in two communities and invited them to discuss and explore having projects all around the neighborhoods for one week. I met with about 15 of them individually and proposed the neighborhood missions. In April 2005, several leaders from 12 different churches came for our first group meeting. I was surprised to see how many were interested since a pastor in my church told me it would be impossible to bring churches of different denominations to work together. It seems strange, but that's reality.

FHL Week 2005 - First prayer walk

FHL Week 2005 - Free carwash

FHL Week 2006 - Second prayer walk,
Indianapolis' Monument Circle

FHL Week 2006 - Merlin encourages
Carmel volunteers

FHL Week (2007) – Volunteers painting
school curbs

FHL Week 2011 - Church beautification

Seven pastors from different denominations committed to do a week of outreaches in our neighborhood. We met on a regular basis identifying needs and resources in our communities. Once we narrowed down the needs list, we developed projects and then asked our congregations and the surrounding businesses to provide the resources needed. We did not have any budget so we worked hard to find resources around us. Seven churches and 200+ volunteers performed 10 projects for the first Faith Hope and Love (FHL) Week in Indianapolis.

I was very happy to see a vision became a reality. By November of the same year some of the pastors who joined us called me and asked what we would be doing the following year. I told them I was done. However, they shared with me that their congregations had a great experience and were already looking forward to next year's local mission. So I developed a plan of action how to share the concept with other communities in metropolitan Indianapolis.

After prayers and encouragement, I shared the vision with several pastors in greater Indianapolis and asked them to be the area coordinators in their communities. The idea seemed very workable and the Lord gave me favor to recruit four more communities to do what is now known as "Mission Trip in Your Own Backyard." The following year, we mobilized 50+ churches and organizations with 1,200 volunteers who performed more than 30 projects during the entire Faith Hope and Love Week.

To date, this ministry has worked with more than 200 different churches crossing denominational lines in central Indiana. FHL has year-round ministries such as planting self-sustained food pantries, Kindness Days and leadership training. It mobilizes more than 3,000 unique volunteers on an annual basis.

FHL and Samaritan's Feet

FHL and IUPUI volunteers clean-up

FHL with Northview Church and
Keep Indianapolis Beautiful

God has been waiting for us to take the land—our neighborhoods and our cities are meant to be habitations of people who will expand the Kingdom of God. We need to become aware of the resources that God had scattered around us. Yes, there are giants in our communities, but God said to be strong and courageous because He will lead us to inherit the land He swore to our forefathers. God will fulfill whatever He promised, even though our circumstance may reflect otherwise. Between our vision and its reality is a gap that may include challenges and will require perseverance on our part. That's our next topic.

God will fulfill whatever He promised,
even though our circumstance may reflect otherwise.

———

## Encountering God

In these hard economic times, have you questioned yourself or God if you have missed the purpose of your life? You thought you were doing what God had called you to do and yet most people you know, even your own family, doubt you. But in spite of all the criticism, you continued on. And things got worse and the rest of the world thought you were a failure.

I have experienced battles within myself and outside of myself about God calling me to start a ministry to bring the unity of the Body of Christ in central Indiana. It is a ministry to encourage and disciple people to walk in their passion while bringing transformation in the neighborhoods.

On October 22, 2003, I had a vivid dream. In the dream, I encountered a big, tall and strong man wearing Middle Eastern clothes. He clearly told me that the answer is between Chapter 16 and18. I knew in my dream that I was dreaming and did not want to forget what the man told me. So I started screaming in my dream, "Chapter 17, Chapter 17, Chapter 17…" Then I woke up with my wife Annie shaking my arm and telling me to wake up. She asked me why I was screaming Chapter 17 over and over again. I told her about the dream, but we didn't know what to make of it. The next morning, Annie told me that she was at a Bible study the night before and they were studying John 17. *My prayer is not for them alone. I pray also for those who will believe in me through their message, that all of them may be one, Father, just as you are in me and I am in you. May they also be in us so that the world may believe that you have sent me. I have given them the glory that you gave me, that they may be one as we are one— I in them and you in me—so that they may be brought to complete unity. Then the world will know that you sent me and have loved them even as you have loved me*" (John 17:20-23). We did not know what to do with the verses until after the first FHL Week. Then I realized that I had encountered God through my dream! "*…so that they may be brought to complete unity. Then the world will know that you sent me and have loved them even as you have loved me.*" Perhaps this dream was what kept me going the past several years even though there were and still are challenges along the way.

God called the prophet Jeremiah while he was still a young man. Maybe he doubted because he did not have a lot of experience in life and in public speaking. He had no extensive background in dealing with the economy and the political arena...and working with the religious people. Nor did he have a lot of money to support his own ministry, and he questioned God of his calling.

In Jeremiah Chapter 15, he doubted God of his assignment. In Chapter 20, he accused God of misleading him. The people made fun of him; they tried to trap him so they could get rid of him. Jeremiah even cursed the day he was born, because his *"entire life has been filled with trouble, sorrow and shame"* (20:18). Can you relate with him making the wrong decisions, feeling like you're bringing down your entire family to destruction because your ministry is a failure? And yet Jeremiah obeyed God and fulfilled his ministry. He encountered the Living God. Despite the criticism and abuse he was going through, he fulfilled his calling and became one of the great prophets of the Old Testament. Jeremiah remained faithful, undeterred by the continuous hardships and disappointments.

## The parallels: Jeremiah's world

During Jeremiah's time, the people lost their freedom and they lost their trust in God. They turned to idols for many years thinking God would not be able to rescue them because of the calamities that were happening. First, they were under the rule of Egypt and later under Babylon when King Nebuchadnezzar defeated Egypt's Pharaoh Necho at Carchemish. Jeremiah's ministry extends over a very critical time in the history of the ancient Middle East. During his time, many people lost their jobs and their properties. They were in debt and inflation was very high. Many people became hungry, which resulted in people becoming selfish.

Because of the economic situation, the "leaders" of that time trusted in their own strength. They devised worldly plans and tried using their power and influence to turn around their nation. They manipulated the people to their own advantage.

Because of military and social unrest, the people turned to idols and that's when Jeremiah came into the picture going against the grain. The Scripture recorded Jeremiah's proclamation of judgment, his prayers, confessions and his relationship with God. He was aware of the idolatry in the land and he preached the covenant of God with His people. Faithfulness with God would bring blessings, but disobedience has consequences– punishment and destruction. Jeremiah saw the corruption in the leaders and witnessed the nation disintegrate morally. Eventually, they brought the entire nation to disaster and people were exiled.

## Our world today

Many of us can relate with the people during Jeremiah's time. We question if we can trust the government system. Because of the economic situation of our country, some of churches and para-churches feel like they're failing because their budgets have been drastically reduced.

Bible study groups wrestle with the signs of the time—the wars that have been going on around the world, 9/11, the earthquakes in Central and South America, the flooding in the Asian countries, the Tsunami in Japan, the recent hurricanes that have flooded and devastated Louisiana and the gulf coast, and the economic challenges that are sweeping the globe.

Recently, one of the major TV networks tackled the critical question, 'Is the United States headed toward bankruptcy?' If things continue to get worse, the country may be headed toward the direction of long term debt and deficit, paralyzing any chance of economic recovery.

More and more people are now resorting to the worldly standards. Our media and arts and entertainment reflect our way of living. Newspapers are dominated by negativity and the evil around us. Many TV reality shows are a mirror of our habits, mentality and the way we live. Unfortunately, these forms of entertainment saturate the minds of viewers to accept immorality, violence and evil as the natural way of living. A quick look at these forms of entertainment reveal that our values have been lost and this is what is now influencing the world. Is this one of the reasons why there is more crime and corruption in our neighborhoods?

Jeremiah's world was not much different than our world today. The majority of us have been influenced and affected by the world's view. We have become a generation that tolerates injustice, sex before marriage, individualism and hypocrisy.

I had the opportunity to volunteer for a prison ministry for about two years. I've been to maximum-security prisons and met inmates who had been in prison for more than 50 years and serving two life terms. I have met young men who are as gentle as a dove and ended up in prison because of stupid mistakes. They grew up in an environment of selfishness, individualism and survival. They knew right from wrong, but their mentality was, who cares.

A few years ago through Faith Hope and Love, Bob Irvin began Jehoshua House, a ministry for ex-offenders to help them re-enter society. Through this ministry, I have had the opportunity to get to know a few ex-offenders. One man was incarcerated for more than 25 years. He attended our men's Bible study group for many months.

After getting "outside" and being exposed to his new environment, he mentioned that he was having a hard time recognizing Christians from non-Christians because they act and behave the same way. He told us that, in prison, if a person identifies himself as a Christian, that person had better be ready to behave as a Christian and live out his faith—or pay the consequences. Under the vigilant eyes of fellow inmates in such a stark environment, there is nothing to hide behind. Who you are is under great scrutiny. If you claim to be a Christian, this means you must follow the principles and the teachings of the Bible. Your words and actions had better reflect your beliefs; otherwise, you will be condemned and beaten by fellow inmates because of your hypocrisy. You would be considered untrustworthy, someone who could turn around and betray others.

That was an enlightening conversation for me. How many times have we jokingly said, "Put on your Sunday smiles and attitudes." We have tolerated the habit of leaving our Christianity at the church on Sunday and living our lives like the rest of the world. As lights of the world, we have to demonstrate our belief through our actions every day, anywhere. Christians need to be the influencers rather than the influenced. How can we change the direction of our generation and help usher in the Kingdom if we act like the rest of the unbelieving world?

Christians need to be the influencers
rather than the influenced.

---

**Grassroots movement in the Kingdom**

Many of us would agree that relationship is the key to transformation. Relationships take time; it means investing our life into another through our actions, values and ideals. In other words, transformation through ministry has to be relational instead of imposing programs that are directed by a few people at the top.

Some reporters and writers recorded that the 2012 drought was the worst in more than half a century. In Indiana, July 2012 was the warmest ever in recorded history. Some say this drought was the fifth worst since 1895. And it may have longer-term effects than we think. Basically, everything eats corn—humans, animals and our vehicles. Because of less vegetation, we will see higher prices on meat since cows, pigs, chicken, sheep, etc., eat corn and other vegetation. Fuel (especially the biofuels and ethanol) costs will increase and the effect will trickle down to many consumables.

Unfortunately, the folks who are at the lower end of the economic scale will suffer the most because their necessities demand a higher percentage of their income. The poor were already hit hard by the recent economic downturn. Then this drought made it worse, which means they have less money to spend on other things such as housing/rent, utilities, fuel, clothing, education, transportation, insurance and health issues. In addition, the U.S. has and may continue in months to come to experience stagnant wages. We have to prepare for the "winter" and the coming challenges in the next few years.

In Genesis Chapter 41, God gave Joseph the warning about the famine through Pharaoh. He immediately responded with wisdom and action. It is now time for us to act and not wait. The army of God needs to rise up once again and be the catalysts and agents of reformation. Our society is hungry and thirsty for what makes sense. If only we can increase the knowledge that the Kingdom of God has all the answers to all our problems, our world would be a better place for all creation.

Food pantry serving fresh vegetables.

Food pantry preparing bags of groceries.

Pantry of Faith.

There are countless ways to bring the awareness of the Kingdom to our neighborhoods. One of them is to multiply the resources needed through the process of reproducing ministries that work. One example is the food pantry planting movement that brings the Kingdom principles into action, as we have done through Faith Hope and Love. It challenges groups of people to partner with several organizations and churches to serve those in need. Each food pantry is comprised of many groups of people such as outreach, prayer and usher teams. Our agreement with the potential partner is to provide them food, volunteers and training for 6 to 9 months, and after that they need to be self-sustained. This means that within that initial training period, they must establish their volunteer system and be connected with food supplies and partners in their communities. This process urges them to take action to get connected and start relationships in their neighborhoods, encourage others to participate, and continue to learn how to be active in a community. In addition, we highly encourage them to help start and establish other food pantries once they've become self-sustained. This system was designed to integrate a more personal touch and more time spent one on one, not only with the clients, but also with other workers or volunteers. This is similar to what Joshua and his troops did to conquer the land of Canaan, but without blood and violence. It is a peaceful invasion of God's people taking action and living out the teachings of Jesus. Our main weapons are not spears or swords, but the unconditional love of God for all humanity expressed in many different ways.

The overall effect is the possibility of getting to know the recipients, neighborhoods, and businesses in their area and to have relationships with them. This opens up opportunities to share the Gospel (Mark 16:15-18) and to pray for them also. These pantries do not hold the clients hostage; they still receive food even if they refuse to be prayed for or to listen to the Gospel. The food pantry workers are instructed to not judge non-believers, but simply extend the love of Christ to them.

Ironically, some of the best volunteers have come from those who first refused to be prayed for because they were not judged.

It is a peaceful invasion of God's people taking action
and living out the teachings of Jesus.

Sadly, I've seen some food pantries that use outreach to increase the number of their membership. The goal is not to increase a church's attendance, but to increase the love of God in the neighborhoods. Once people see the non-judgment and the unconditional love for them, they make decisions to stay connected with the church. By actually experiencing the love of God for them in tangible ways, they normally get attracted to what Christianity is all about. Because of the sense of belonging, there are more opportunities to encourage them to become volunteers and advocates as well. Enabling people is better than making them dependent on others. Making people feel appreciated and dignified instead of humiliated is a way to increase their morale that could lead them to live a more productive life.

In my experience I have found that through the food pantry planting principle, more volunteers are mobilized or discipled (Matt. 28:18-20) than with other ministry programs. This model spurs the idea of planting many smaller food pantries rather than having just a few large ones. What tends to happen with large food pantries is that they become more food-directed than people-directed, and relationships become second to food, which can be counter-productive. Because of long lines in larger food pantries, volunteers tend to give the bags of food without much interaction with recipients. The end result is that people come back for food, not for their newfound friends. However, there are larger food pantries that are very effective in recruiting more volunteers to cater to people on a personal level.

The grassroots ministry approach results in more people reaching out for the available resources in communities, which means a higher success rate of becoming self-sustained. They literally become equipped to stand on their own feet in due time. Many of the clients become volunteers because it is encouraged from the very start. They tend to have a sense of ownership and a vested interest in keeping it going. Their value as individuals rises and they tell more people about it.

The domino effect starts to happen. Since there are more volunteers who have a sense of ownership in the pantry, more people are mobilized to reach out for Christ. Thus, the opportunity to preach the Gospel and to disciple the nation can move forward on a rapid scale.

In Acts 6, the early disciples recognized the need to provide food for the disadvantaged. At that time, the early church was growing fast; however, as it grew, the challenges multiplied. There was a certain group of widows who felt they were neglected in the food distribution. The apostles realized they needed to attend to the physical needs, but they couldn't abandon prayers and the teaching of the Word.

They decided to identify a team of people to run their food pantry. The result was that the Word of God prospered and the church grew even more rapidly. I believe that during each food distribution, Stephen and his team presented the Gospel and loved on people. Because of the combination of service and the sharing of the Word, more relationships happened, belonging was obvious, and thus the church increased in size even more rapidly. I would also venture to say that the "clients" became volunteers and advocates for the cause.

Attend to the physical needs of the people (Acts 6:1-7), preach the Gospel (Mark 16:15) and disciple the nation (Matthew 28:19) are the values that make this simple concept effective in many ways. It is about creating an atmosphere that invites the power of God to invade the hearts of the people. Some people may say there are too many food pantries around. The Bible says that there will always be poor in the land. This means that we can never have enough food pantries in our cities. We just need to increase the love in the neighborhoods that will foster trust and relationships. Authentic relationships produce integrity in everyone, which means there will be more trust in the system for both parties—encouragement instead of judgment, honesty instead of taking advantage of others, and community instead of strife.

These food pantries become channels of blessings, a network of relationships and interdependent self-sufficient communities.

*During this time some prophets traveled from Jerusalem to Antioch. One of them named Agabus stood up in one of the meetings and predicted by the Spirit that a great famine was coming upon the entire Roman world. (This was fulfilled during the reign of Claudius.) So the believers in Antioch decided to send relief to the brothers and sisters in Judea, everyone giving as much as they could. This they did, entrusting their gifts to Barnabas and Saul to take to the elders of the church in Jerusalem* (Acts 11:27-30, NLT).

Another aspect of the food pantry planting movement is to help each other in times of crisis and need. For example, if a tornado hit the east side of town and people needed help, we could call on the other pantries in that area to help them out with physical and spiritual assistance. As Christians, we are called to bring solutions to the world's problems. This grassroots movement can transform one locality at a time; it is simple, it makes sense, it is practical and answers the needs in our neighborhoods.

## Communication in the Kingdom

When we are in a battle we don't see everything, but we can always look to Jesus first. That's why the prophet Jeremiah said, *"Let's not leave the fountain of living water and go to the broken cisterns for fresh water."* Our first job is to seek God and our questions and problems in life will be answered. God is the fountain of fresh flowing water.

On July 29, 2004, the Lord gave me a very significant dream. This was during the time that our home group in the upper room had been studying the Book of Acts and was experiencing the power of the Holy Spirit, and we were wanting more! This dream was symbolic of what happened in the coming days and weeks.

At that time, I was reading *The Radical Middle* to help me in my studies with the Vineyard Leadership Institute. I had such a hunger to know more! I was intrigued about what was happening in Toronto, Canada, with the POWER of the Holy Spirit. The Lord was working in mighty ways there! People from all over the world were empowered by the Holy Spirit when they visited and when they went home that POWER went with them! The spirit flowed from them to their church or ministry! It became known as The Toronto Blessing.

The Holy Spirit began stirring in my heart to go there. I asked Annie to research the church and she found the Toronto Airport Christian Fellowship (now Catch the Fire) website. I took over and found a conference that was happening the week of September 7, 2004, called Fresh Anointing. But we found out it was in Spanish and it would cost $75 each! There was no way we could go; besides, we did not understand Spanish! But that night the Lord gave me a dream that we just could not ignore!

*In the dream, I was by a riverbank and I saw a large, old sailboat. Its fishing net was in the water. I thought to myself, "He is going to catch a lot of fish since he is the only one fishing in the river!"*

*Then, I found myself in his boat and as he pulled in the fishing net, I saw many different kinds of fish. He carefully rinsed them individually, squeezing each one of them gently to make sure they were clean. Most of the fish were about 6 to 8 inches long. I noticed that some were in the bucket ready to be cooked; he had already cleaned out their guts.*

*I asked the fisherman where we were going and he said that we were going to Canada. He said that there's a small body of water there. In the middle of it is a fountain of liquid gold! The fisherman said that the owner of the body of water gives it away free since it is endless. At that time, I could see in my mind that it was like a hot spring with a place bubbling up golden water. Suddenly, my wife Annie was in the boat wandering around the ship picking up jars. I asked her what she was doing and she said she was looking for empty jars so we could bring the liquid gold back home.*

As soon as I woke up I told Annie about my dream. We were so excited! She had me tell it to her again and told me the Lord was giving me a message through my dream! She had me write it down and we asked the Lord for revelation about its message. Annie told me that she believed the liquid gold represented the gift of the Holy Spirit and the Lord was calling me to be a fisher of men.

Annie got on the computer and told me, "You are not going to believe this, but the conference is now FREE!" Wow! In the dream the liquid gold was FREE! I couldn't deny that the Lord was speaking to me! That was a confirmation for us to pursue our plan to attend. Revelation 21:6 says, *I will give of the fountain of the water of life freely to him who thirsts,* further affirming that God had been communicating with us. We were destined to be in Toronto.

It gets better. In my dream, I was in a fishing boat with a person who caught a lot of fish of different kinds and sizes. This portion of the dream would later reveal my calling to proclaim the message of salvation, *"Come follow me,"* Jesus said, *"and I will make you fishers of men"* (Matthew 4:19).

Well, we could not wait to tell our home group about how God was speaking through the dream. We told them we would be going and two others from our group wanted to come with us. So we prepared for our road trip to Toronto for the Fresh Anointing conference. When we walked in, the worship had already begun. You could feel the Lord's presence there! The songs were in Spanish, but it did not matter. It was as if our spirit knew what we were singing. There was a dynamic Argentine speaker, but there was also an English interpreter who was equally expressive.

At the end of the multi-day conference, the pastor of the church, John Arnott, spoke about the Holy Spirit and how we are carriers of Him. He said that we need to continually be filled up with the Holy Spirit so that He will overflow from us to others. If we keep it to ourselves we cannot bless others. John asked if we wanted to receive more of the Holy Spirit. Of course, who wouldn't want more? So he asked us to symbolically hold up our hands as if we were holding a jar. That's right, he said a JAR—just like in my dream! Annie and I looked at each other and our friends and began to laugh! We held up our jars and we could actually feel the presence of the Lord.

John asked everyone to call out where they were from. There were people from all over the world and just a few from the U.S. When it was our turn we said that we were from Indianapolis. As John continued to speak he kept looking at Annie and me, and also our two friends. I turned to Annie and said, "I have a feeling he is going to call us up." He would speak and then pause slightly as he looked at us. Then, out of hundreds of people in the sanctuary, he said, "You four in the sixth row from Indianapolis, come on up. The Lord has a blessing for you!" We jumped up with anticipation for what the Lord would do next and ran up onto the stage! John said, "God wants to give you a triple portion! Hold up your jars." I don't know how it happened, but before I knew what I was doing, I had the microphone in my hand and told John, "I saw this in a dream and I didn't come with a jar... I brought my barrel!" Then John went to place his hand on our foreheads to pray for us, but before he even touched us we could feel the power and presence of the Holy Spirit! This experience was awe-inspiring! God fulfilled what He conveyed in my dream and during the next few months He began to work through me in a more powerful way!

God communicates with us in many different ways, such as dreams and visions. Make sure to listen carefully and obey God when He speaks to you. Look to Jesus first. He also communicates with us through others, such as prophets.

Another way we can communicate with God is through our prayers. One day during the first week of October 2012, we brought 23 volunteers to help out a person who was not able to do strenuous physical activities because of illness. This person did not ask for help, but I was prompted by the Holy Spirit to bring volunteers to provide assistance. We cleaned the area around the home, built a chicken coop, power-washed the deck, made a small wood fence, cleaned gutters and did other chores inside the house. After a few days of outreach, the person wrote that prayers were answered. This person had been praying for a group of volunteers to help because of physical health.

One weekend every fall, a church in Carmel, Indiana, closes its weekend services to encourage the entire congregation to serve the community. They serve several neighborhoods and work with a number of non-profit organizations. On October 13-14, 2012, our ministry received about 250 volunteers from them to work on two projects. Several of the groups were assigned to our ongoing project called Heal the Land, a neighborhood cleanup near downtown Indianapolis.

Before we gave instructions for the neighborhood cleanup, I shared with them that cleaning the streets is only secondary to their collective presence and prayers in the area. Since we have God in our hearts, we can also release His presence wherever we are. I encouraged them to do prayer walks as well. We prayed together before we started the cleanup. This particular outreach site is in a tough neighborhood with prostitution and drug problems. It seems like many of the residents (and/or the residents near the area) do not care for their surroundings since they have a chronic problem of trashing the alleys and the vacant and abandoned lots. We have been bringing volunteers to this same area for almost two years on a regular basis with some progress. However, we believe that God wants to heal this land.

After a few hours of cleanup we gathered together for testimonials and debriefing. One of the stories was about a couple who badly needed assistance clearing and cleaning their backyard. The lady of the house was 81 years old. Their backyard was full of overgrown weeds and all kinds of trash. After one of the volunteers prayed for them, I had the opportunity to interview the man of the house. He said that the same morning, he was fasting and asking God to send help for his yard. He almost broke down in tears when one of the groups showed up in his backyard that afternoon. His prayers reached God and He got his answer immediately!

We ended the debriefing with prayer. Bill, our project manager, was leading the prayer in front of about 70 volunteers on the side of a street when I noticed a woman walking in front of me. She looked depressed and she looked surprised that a bunch of people in her neighborhood were praying together on the street. I continued to pray and forgot about the woman. After a few minutes of prayer, all the volunteers left. As I was gathering our tools, I saw the same woman being prayed for by Bill and Donna. She came back and spilled her heart to them. God had convicted her to come back to us instead of pursuing her plan to shoplift. She was going to help herself to cleaning supplies for her apartment at a nearby grocery store because she was going to be evicted into the streets in the next few days. She had a black eye and backache because her boyfriend beat her and left her. She did not have anyone in her life because her children were taken away from her a number of years ago while she was in jail. She was scheduled to appear in court the following week because of her habitual shoplifting. Bill and Donna prayed for her and led her to the Lord. I asked her if I could put spit on her black eye while I prayed for healing. She hesitantly agreed and within a minute of prayer she said her eye was not hurting anymore. Bill and Donna ended up buying her clothes, supplies and food.

*As soon as you began to pray, a word went out, which I have come to tell you, for you are highly esteemed* (Daniel 9:23). We need to focus on God first; He has all the answers. God had heard the prayers earlier that day for the couple who needed help in their backyard, for the woman in desperation, and for our group to be a part of what He is doing in that neighborhood. God communicates with us all the time.

## If, then, maybe and perhaps

We tend to go through life tuned out. We become like zombies programmed by our society. It's typical to follow the crowd without questioning those in front of us. Our culture molds our minds and behavior through many channels such as fashion, tradition and trends. But God communicates with us all the time too; we just need to tune in and be aware of His promptings. He speaks to us in countless ways such as dreams, visions, signs and wonders, pets (or donkeys), life situations, music, people on the street, even non-Christians, and just regular people. In the Old and New Testament, the Lord chooses to communicate frequently to His people through the prophets to deliver messages, warnings and instructions.

*Gather before judgment begins, before your time to repent is blown away like chaff. Act now, before the fierce fury of the Lord falls and the terrible day of the Lord's anger begins. Seek the Lord, all who are humble, and follow his commands. Seek to do what is right and to live humbly. Perhaps even yet the Lord will protect you—protect you from his anger on that day of destruction* (Zephaniah 2:2-3).

In this instance, God sent the prophets as His messengers to warn the people what was decreed in heaven. There is a term called "prophetic clause." The prophetic clause is dependent on the response of the people. It is an "if-then" clause, which means that through our response, the decree can change and we can have an alternate future. God sees from heaven what has been going on in the world such as injustice, crime, hunger and other forms of evil. He sees how His people react, good or bad, ardor or apathy. God intervenes to bring His Kingdom, but as verse 3 states, we need to seek the Lord, do what is right, live humbly and "perhaps" He would protect us when He brings judgment.

A good example is the story of Sodom and Gomorrah. God sent two angels to execute His judgment on the people. Even the angels experienced the heinousness of the people when they were inside Lot's house. *Meanwhile, the angels questioned Lot, "Do you have any other relatives here in the city?" they asked. "Get them out of this place—your sons-in-law, sons, daughters, or anyone else. For we are about to destroy this city completely. The outcry against this place is so great it has reached the Lord, and he has sent us to destroy it"* (Gen 19:12-13 (NLT). The story continued with the angels helping Lot, granting his request to go to a small village rather than escaping to the mountains. The angel did not destroy the small village and everyone with Lot was saved except his wife who disobeyed the order and turned into a pillar of salt.

As I mentioned in the earlier part of the book, many of our neighborhoods are deteriorating physically, morally and spiritually. We have more hungry and homeless in our neighborhoods than any time in our history. Crimes and injustices are happening at an accelerated rate around us. It has been said that slavery is more rampant now than before the civil war. Human trafficking is the modern form of slavery where people profit from the control and exploitation of others, which affects an estimated 700,000 to 2 million people around the globe each year. Thousands of victims land in the United States. An estimated 3,700 abortions happen in the U.S. every day. According to Wikipedia, from Oct. 1, 2008, to Sept. 30, 2009, roughly 1 out of 200 persons in the U.S. used a shelter system at some point during that period.

God is shaking our land with justice. He does not like injustices for He is a just God. He will bring calamity and disasters to make things right. The injustices, rebellion and compromise are blatantly evident in our neighborhoods. God will not tolerate apathy and conformity. He will bring judgment to earth, but He is also coming with His mercy for those who listen and obey His words. *If I announce that a certain nation or kingdom is to be uprooted, torn down, and destroyed, but then that nation renounces its evil ways, I will not destroy it as I had planned. And if I announce that I will plant and build up a certain nation or kingdom, but then that nation turns to evil and refuses to obey me, I will not bless it as I said I would.* (Jer. 18:7-10). God's action is consistent with His nature, which is holy and just. He will punish the deceivers and will reward those who are living out their faith in Him.

As God releases His message to His people, He also provides them with warnings and ways to change their manner of living as we have seen in Genesis 19. He is slow to anger and abounding in love, but there's a point in time when He brings His judgment to earth. However, if a nation or a community changes its actions, perhaps the Lord will protect them when He brings judgment in that area.

The opportunities in our midst to demonstrate His love are endless. We need only open our eyes to see the needs in our neighborhoods so we can provide assistance and answers for them. Acts 10:38b Jesus *"went around doing good."* Jesus not only preached the Gospel—He also went around doing outreaches and demonstrating the power of God.

We cannot continue to stand still and wait for others to address the injustices and the sin around us. Rather, we need to be active participants to bring transformation in our communities through the tangible acts of love, mercy and service. God will not tolerate apathy and disobedience. He wants us to pray and to provide solutions to the problems. He wants His people to come back to Him and to continue the works of Jesus here on earth. He wants us to usher the coming of His Kingdom through unity in the Spirit.

We cannot continue to stand still and wait for others
to address the injustices and the sin around us.

———

It is easy to abandon our faith in God when the world is saying you are a failure. I believe this is a reminder to us that we need to put our faith in the Spring of Living Water. It is easy to blame one another and point fingers at each other. Back biting is not of God, but of the devil. God wants His children to be united. *Their responsibility is to equip God's people to do his work and build up the church, the body of Christ. This will continue until we all come to such unity in our faith and knowledge of God's Son that we will be mature in the Lord, measuring up to the full and complete standard of Christ* (Ephesians 4:12-13, NLT). It is our job to build up one another. We have to work together since not one person or organization has it all. As we network and labor together, each of us is strengthened through and by one another because of our uniqueness. Some of us may be good at teaching while others are good at providing practical, hands-on assistance. Joined together, we become the Body of Christ in our cities. Our churches become The Church of the city with many different locations, but all communicating the same message.

When we come together in unity, the enemy becomes weaker. His dominion shrinks, growing quieter and less powerful. He has less voice in our communities and the Light of Christ pushes back the darkness. Together, we overcome him by the blood of the Lamb and by the word of our testimonies. Our testimonies are comprised of words and actions that can bring the new consciousness into our surroundings. This new way of living guided by the Bible and through the power of the Holy Spirit can answer all the issues in our cities. God is restoring His creation through us. It is the utmost privilege to be a part of His plan and of His action. He will reveal your calling and He will communicate His will and His plan as long as you are listening intimately to His voice and being aware of His presence.

## A city of hope

Two years ago I met a group of people from Manchester, Kentucky, when they hosted a movie called *The Appalachian Dawn* at a church near Indianapolis. I was hesitant to see the movie, but I was encouraged by my wife and our friend to go. It was a documentary of a small southern Kentucky community that was infested with drugs and crime. For 200 years, there had been unresolved animosity that eventually defiled the land with blood, corruption and injustice. Drug overdoses and violence were a normal way of life in the city. A daughter of the school superintendent and the mayor's sons were involved in illicit drugs. Some of the government officials were actually part of the serious problems. The residents gave up and they lost their hope. Doug Abner, a pastor in Clay County Manchester, stated, "Good people sat back and did nothing...the lack of light was more of the problem than the darkness. Then, God came to town."

When we come together in unity,
the enemy becomes weaker.

———

I was so touched by the documentary that I arranged a two-day visit with the people who were actually involved in the work leading to the breakthrough in this community. What happened there was referred to as the first known modern transformation in a North American community. My group and I met with the town librarian. He was one of the people involved when the breakthrough happened. He introduced us to some of the leaders and pastors who were also involved, and drove us around to point out different places where various events transpired during the wave of God that swept the city.

Out of desperation, the city's pastors had decided they had had enough of the corruption and were willing to come together to repent, pray and to ask the Lord to heal their land. They took it into their own hands and accepted the fact that the government and other institutions did not have the solution to the overwhelming and persistent problems. They had gotten to the point that they were willing to face whatever consequences may happen from their actions.

One night, the Lord gave one of the local pastors a dream. He saw the churches uniting to pray together for God to expose the darkness. On the rainy day of May 2, 2004, 3,500+ people marched together in prayer. The town saw the power of God immediately. Within several days after the prayer walk, God exposed the sources of corruption, which brought national attention. The town's mayor was arrested together with other officials. In his place a new mayor was elected—a Christian who starts each day in prayer with her staff at the city hall. A notorious drug dealer and town brawler received the Lord and became a street evangelist and is now one of the Christian leaders in the city. Due to his change in belief and in his life, more former outlaws came to the Lord. Before the transformation, the rivers and streams were polluted due to the physical and spiritual effects of the events that had transpired there. Many of the wild life species had left the county because of the defilement of the land. Now, the city produces one of the best bottled water in the state of Kentucky. Many residents were addicted to drugs; this presented an opportunity for the city to build a rehab facility. The nation's only Christian-run rehab was built in Manchester, mostly funded by the government through the prayers of the saints. Soon 1,400 new jobs were created in this 1,900-member town.

It was such a blessing for us to visit and speak with the people who had been a part of the wave that God brought to the city. A place that was once a haven for crime, drugs and corruption has been transformed to a place of hope. On the way back to Indianapolis, we saw the sign at the city boundary: "Manchester, City of Hope." It is indeed a city of hope.

What do you see in your world today? Despair or hope, hate or love, fear or joy, chaos or peace? What can you do in your neighborhood in the Name of Jesus? We owe it to the next generation. The decision you make today can change and affect the future of your neighborhoods, your country and the world. Would more people find eternal life because he/she was affected by your decision today?

What will be your legacy? What if we let the Holy Spirit be our Advocate and realize that we have a counselor from heaven? What would our lives be? What if we are the generation that would change the course of history? What would be your part in shaping the future of our world? Would you be a history-maker or a spectator? When you meet our Creator, will He say, "Well done, good and faithful servant"?

How do you see the world in 10 or 20 years from now? What would the world look like if you could say, "The Kingdom of God is here"?

## Our generation

*... And teaching them to obey everything I have commanded you. And surely I am with you always, to the very end of the*

*age"* (Matthew 28:20). Jesus told all His disciples to teach everything He had taught them. Everything means all. This was His mandate to all disciples to teach the next generations, and so on. We are now the generation that has received the mandate of Jesus. We need to obey everything that Jesus taught His disciples in the New Testament.

We need to wake up like Jacob did when he saw that there was an open heaven right in front of Him. When we accept Jesus as our Lord, the King of all Kings, we become His dwelling place. We become carriers of His presence and the Kingdom of God. We need to step out in the reality of the Kingdom and release the delegated power and authority wherever we go. In the first pages of this book, I wrote about Jacob's dream of a stairway that reached from earth to heaven where angels go up and down (Genesis 28). Later, God spoke to Jacob that the ground he was lying on belonged to him. *"I tell you the truth, you will all see heaven open and the angels of God going up and down on the Son of Man, the one who is the stairway between heaven and earth"* (John 1:51, NLT). Jesus is the "Jacob's ladder" to us where angels are going up and down from heaven to earth.

Our neighborhoods are crying out for the Kingdom to come. They are desperate. God is waiting for us; our neighborhoods are waiting for us to operate in the Kingdom reality and the works of God. The world is looking for us Christians to be the miracles in their midst. Many of them are willing and just waiting for someone like you to be a conduit of the awareness of His presence. The opportunity lies in front of us to change the course of history — of a city, a nation and the world.

*Arise, shine, for your light has come, and the glory of the Lord rises upon you* (Isaiah 60:1).

It's your time to arise; you are a part of the army that is rising up! This generation is called to proclaim and demonstrate the Kingdom of God in our cities. You are called and commissioned to expand the Kingdom of God in your neighborhoods, cities, and to the ends of the earth.

Look to Jesus first, then act accordingly. He is the Lord over all creation and history. Get counsel from God first, then work on it. That is why going to church, having Bible study and being in relationship with other Christians is very important. We need to learn from and be encouraged by one another.

As I wrote earlier, the summer of 2012 in Indiana was one of the driest and hottest summers in recorded history. One summer afternoon, my wife and I received complimentary tickets to an outdoor concert. We invited our friend Donna to come with us. The place was packed with more than 5,000 people spread out on the grass under the blazing sun and about 100 degree high humidity weather. We wanted to be close to the front, but almost every space was occupied. My wife spotted an empty space toward the front; it seemed to me that it was reserved. We went for it and started to set down our cooler and chairs. I was happy that we were able to find a place, sat on my comfortable folding chair and got ready for a great 4th of July concert. Suddenly, my wife noticed a lady behind us who was about to pass out because of the heat. Since our friend Donna is a nurse, she asked me to go with her to help the lady. By this time, the lady was unconscious. Donna took charge. She asked me to help her lay the ill woman down with her head lower than her body to stimulate oxygen to flow in her head. As soon as we laid her down we commanded life to her body in Jesus' Name. Suddenly she woke up wondering what was happening. I was amazed at what just happened! People around us began to come over to help, putting wet cloths on her face, ice packs on her neck. Others put an umbrella above her while still others were frantically fanning her face with air. We stayed with her while we waited for the paramedics to come. Fifteen minutes later, they arrived and immediately took her blood pressure, which was dangerously low. It was 60/40 even after 15 minutes of being resuscitated and cooled down with fans, cold water and shade. Donna concluded that her blood pressure must be a lot lower because she passed out. If we were not there to help her, she could have reached a very critical level that could have damaged her brain or even cost her life.

God had "reserved" the space for us next to the person who would need help. We were given an assignment and we were obedient to Him—the rest was His-story. Could it be that "Jacob's ladder" became available to us so that heaven came to bring life to the woman in need?

If the Kingdom is the rule of God, then it should reveal His character and His actions. Jesus modeled this to us while He was here on earth. Just hours before Jesus left this earth, He reminded

His disciples in John 20:21, *"Peace be with you! As the Father has sent me, I am sending you."*

## What does the Kingdom of God look like now?

*Then Jesus asked, "What is the kingdom of God like? What shall I compare it to? It is like a mustard seed, which a man took and planted in his garden. It grew and became a tree, and the birds perched in its branches." Again he asked, "What shall I compare the kingdom of God to? It is like yeast that a woman took and mixed into about sixty pounds of flour until it worked all through the dough"* (Luke 13:18-21).

The Kingdom started with a small band of people that Jesus gathered. During His time, people thought He was crazy and very unusual. The majority did not believe Him. Like a very tiny mustard seed, it did not seem like his ministry could ever grow into a big tree with branches so big they would serve as a roost for the birds. In this world as we know it, mustard seeds do not grow to be a tree, but rather a shrub, but that's based on our cognitive minds. Our logical thinking, trying to fit the supernatural into the natural, hinders many of us. How can we mentally process and describe the infinite and boundless Kingdom with our finite minds? As He did in many parables, Jesus surprised His listeners. How can a mustard seed grow to become a tree? This question is comparable to "How can a man who was pronounced dead and buried in a cave come back to life and walk in front of many witnesses with his body still wrapped in linen and cloth?" The point is that when God is involved, what starts out so tiny can become unbelievably gigantic; His realm will continue to grow and cover the entire earth. When you and I accepted Christ in our hearts, we were commissioned to continue His ministry on earth, to expand His Kingdom. What do you think would happen to our lives if we lived with His perspective?

The parable of the leaven is similar. The yeast works through the bread dough and eventually diffuses through and through. Again, what starts out as a small portion of yeast permeates the entire batch slowly until it is saturated with its presence. The growth was almost not happening, but over time, a pinch of yeast impregnates the dough.

The Kingdom continues to invade our neighborhoods with its power and authority. What we do may seem insignificant, but God takes care of the details. Small things can lead to many open doors of opportunity to bring Heaven on earth. As He makes the seed grow, He causes the earth to be saturated with His Word and actions.

## 10/40 window in our own backyard

In 1990, Luis Bush coined the phrase "10/40 window," which refers to the section of the world that is least reached by the Gospel. These regions have roughly two-thirds of the world's population. Many governments in these countries formally or informally prohibit Christian teachings. Thus, the term "window" was used because of the window of opportunity to evangelize these countries.

According to Wikipedia, approximately 77% of the U.S. population was Christians in 2009, down from 86% in 1990. This should not surprise us since the U.S. has become too secularized in its approach to life. The country that has the motto "In God We Trust" on its currency is now divided in its approach to Christianity. If the trend continues at its current rate, Christians could be the minority in the decades to come. We may be looking at the next 10/40 window right in our own backyard.

My recent conversations with a few local Christian denominational leaders revealed that about 10%-20% of the congregations tithe and are active in the works of the church. This means that about 85% of Christians are church-goers (I heard someone referred to them as half-baked Christians or part-time Christians), but are not actively involved in sharing the Gospel and are not being discipled. In general, who are the Christians in this country? Do they reflect Christ in their lives? Can we easily distinguish a Christian in a crowd? Or is it getting harder and harder to identify them?

In the Old Testament, Moses had the same issue. In Numbers 13 and 14, Moses was instructed by God to send one leader from each of the 12 ancestral tribes. They were to explore the land of Canaan with very specific orders: find out if the people living there are weak or strong, few or many, and find out if the land is fertile. After 40 days of exploration, the men reported that the land was a bountiful country—land flowing with milk and honey. But they also found out that the people living there were powerful and their towns were fortified. Ten out of the twelve men came back with negative reports, trying to convince the entire community not to take the land. They said it would be impossible to conquer it. They would prefer to go back to being slaves again in Egypt or to die in the desert.

After a few thousand years, our society is still the same. There are more negative people than the Calebs and the Joshuas. More people complain and even convince others why it cannot be done even though God has already told them to take the land. More people are willing to go back to the slavery in Egypt than to work hard and take the promise. All twelve spies reported the same information but *only two* believed God and were willing to take the land—that's just 16% who came back with courage to do God's work. Remember earlier the pastors said that, generally, only 10%-20% of the congregation tithes and does the works of the church.

God had promised the people a land flowing with milk and honey. All they had to do was take it. Instead of believing God, they came up with all kinds of excuses and rebelled against God by not taking action. The end of the story was that God granted their wish to rebel; no one in their generation, including Moses, reached the Promised Land except Caleb and Joshua.

Our generation has the responsibility to take action to take the land. Similar to the generation of Moses, the future of the next generation depends on our generation. We are all a part of the history of Christianity in the U.S. and in the world. Our generation can reverse the trend of increasing apathy of the church by taking God for His Word.

The next 10/40 window is not hard to reach—it's the absence of passion in the Christian world that prevents the Gospel from reaching our own backyards. This 10/40 window could empower governments to formally or informally prohibit Christian teachings. The next 10/40 will be marked by the apathy of Christians. Physically, it is right here in our own backyard. Our cities are waiting for the concerted action of Christians to take the land. Instead of the darkness that continues to expand, the light of Christ can cover the land with the Calebs and the Joshuas.

Currently, the Calebs and Joshuas are still the minority. The good news is that they can be like the yeast or the mustard seed. They have the influence to wake up the rest of the church. They do not deny the giants and the fortified cities. In fact, they actually are excited that they will advance to occupy the land. They know the giants will be their prey because the giants have no protection. They recognize that God will bring them to safety and will give the land to them as He had promised.

Our generation should see what Caleb and Joshua saw. We need to have the same heart that will not settle for less. The giants of crime, sex, drugs and injustice are no match against the God we serve; they will fall prey to us. We need to see these circumstances as "windows" of opportunity. We cannot sit too long in the pews, but rather must follow the examples of Jesus who spent more of his time outside the synagogues. We are to survey and explore the land. Find out the needs and the available resources in our neighborhoods. Check out the soil to see if it is fertile and rich. What are the traditions and culture surrounding our churches? Out of this information, we need to process them the right way; otherwise, we may stumble onto the wrong path that the majority of spies took in Moses' time—they evaluated the situation erroneously and convinced not only themselves but the rest of the population against the will of God. They rebelled against God by not taking action. God has given us the promise of abundant life. He commanded us to take the land. You and I are a part of God's plan to reach out to our communities, to preach the Gospel and to disciple nations.

## Living on a higher level

Jesus said in Matthew 11:11, *"I tell you the truth: Among those born of women there has not risen anyone greater than John the Baptist; yet he who is least in the kingdom of heaven is greater than he."*

Jesus said that the least in the Kingdom is greater than John the Baptist. Does it mean that we who are in Christ are greater than the OT prophets? How about Abraham, Noah, Moses, Joshua, David, Daniel and Elijah? Yes, yes, yes...you and me! Whether you are from Indianapolis or even from the Philippines! Jesus is counting on us before He comes back. We are His plan. John the baptist was the forerunner of the inauguration of the Kingdom here on earth. We live in-between the times; the Kingdom here on earth now...a present reality and the consummation of the Kingdom of God at the second coming of Christ. This means that in Christ's new covenant, we enjoy the benefits of the Kingdom life. We live on a higher level than anyone before Christ came to this earth. Don't be fooled by the world's theories that miracles don't happen anymore. You and I are the miracles that the world is waiting for. The world needs to be aware that the Kingdom is within us. The Kingdom is in our midst. We need to apprehend it and to live out our faith.

Look around your neighborhood. Does it reflect the Rule of God or the rule of man? Revelation 11:15 says, *The kingdoms of this world have become the kingdoms of our Lord and of His Christ, and He shall reign forever and ever!* That's where we are heading. You can choose if you want to stay on the sidelines or be an active participant.

The season of change and the manifestation of the Kingdom are upon us. God is making all things new. He is shifting things according to what's written in the Scriptures. We are to press in and to take what belongs to us. We are active participants in the transformation of the kingdoms of this world. It is a privilege, an honor and a grace from God that we have a part in the process of redemption of the fallen world. However, it is up to you and me to decide to use the power and authority God has given us through His Holy Spirit. We are individually accountable to God for the renewal of our cities. We are responsible to the future of our children and to the preservation of earth that was handed to us since Adam and Eve. God wants us to take the land He has promised to us. He wants us to live out our birthright—we are heirs of the Kingdom.

You and I can be a portal where the world can access heaven's resources through our relationship with Christ. *"For indeed, the kingdom of God is within you"* (Luke 17:21, NKJV).

As we conclude, I pray that God will grant all of us the grace to be aware of the power and authority that Jesus promised to all of us. I pray that in the midst of trials God will make us aware of the reality of the Kingdom similar to Jacob when he saw the ladder with angels going up and down to heaven. I pray that we will become aware of the spiritual realm in our midst very much like Elisha when he saw the hills full of horses and chariots of fire (2 Kings 6:16-17). I pray that the paradox of the Kingdom will be revealed to us such as Paul preaching freedom while he was in prison, and Christ speaking life while He was about to be crucified. I pray that we will resolve to be strong and courageous like Joshua. I pray that our faith and devotion would be like King David when he killed Goliath with a sling. I pray that we will multiply our talents as the Master expects. I pray that our relationship with Jesus would be as His relationship with the Father. I pray John 17:23-24 that we will be in complete unity in Christ. I pray, "May Your Kingdom come, may Your will be done on earth as it is in Heaven." I pray that your life will reflect the presence of the Kingdom, *"because the kingdom of God is in your midst"* (Luke 17:21).

## QUESTIONS FOR STUDY

1. Have you ever had a dream and didn't have the money to make it happen, but in spite of the money issue you went ahead in faith? Did you realize your dream? What was the most important thing you learned? Where do you draw the line when your financial statement won't allow you to move forward and do the things you sense are the Lord's will?

   _____

   _____

   _____

   _____

2. Read Psalm 145:4-6. It's our obligation to tell the story of the glorious wonders of our God in our lives. In the next 14 days, keep track of your awareness of the works of God in your life and your reaction to the world around you. Were your thoughts and awareness dominated by God or by your circumstances? What influences your perspective? Do you tend to talk more about the goodness of God or your life struggles? What one thing would you work on to increase your consciousness of God in your midst?

   _____

   _____

   _____

   _____

3.  *For as he thinks in his heart, so is he* (Proverb 23:7, NKJV). Identify traditions and beliefs that are holding you back from pursuing your higher calling. List each of them and write how each affects you mentally and physically. What are the limiting thoughts and how will you overcome them? How are you going to change your attitude toward customs and habits that are limiting you in experiencing God?

    _____

    _____

    _____

    _____


4.  Read Jeremiah 15:10-21 and 20:7-18, and Matthew 14:22-32. What are the similarities between Jeremiah and Peter? Most of us can relate to both of them at some point in our lives—the blending of the mountaintop and the deep valley experience, faith and doubt. If we are to follow the Lord, we have to continue to grow. Identify at least 2 areas in your life that God is dealing with you currently. What action steps would you do to continue to grow your faith walk with Jesus?

    _____

    _____

    _____

    _____

5.  The Bible records that God speaks to us in many different ways, including visions, dreams, audible words and life circumstances. Read Acts 10:9-48. Have you had similar situations as Peter or Cornelius? How did you react and did you follow through? What can you do to sharpen your senses and your spirit to hear the voice of God even more?

    _____

    _____

    _____

    _____

6.  Psalm 133, John 17:20-24 and Ephesians 4:12-13 talk about unity and being one in the spirit. What do you think are the stumbling blocks in the unity of believers? What are 5 things you can do to bring unity in the body of Christ? Based on Ephesians 4, what is a mature Christian? How can you apply these principles to help you stay on course in your Christian walk? In the next 2 weekends, have a meeting with Christians from different denominations to discuss potential inter-denominational projects.

    _____

    _____

    _____

    _____

7. Read Matthew 13. Based on these Kingdom principles, how can you protect yourself from the traps of the devil in pursuing your passion? Which parable would empower you to your quest for the Kingdom of God? What do you think would happen to our lives if we lived with His perspective?

_____

_____

_____

_____

8. The new "10/40 window" has been crippling society in the U.S. for many years now due to apathy slowly invading our cities. How do you think it started? What practical things can you do to reverse the trend of this 10/40 window in the U.S. and in your own community?

_____

_____

_____

_____

9. This book was written not only to give you information and to share powerful stories but also to encourage you to take action to live out your faith. Throughout the book, you have read stories of identifying resources and how volunteers came together to address needs. Read Numbers 13:6-30. Conceptualize a project/event based on the needs in your community, then form a team to assist you in the implementation. As a followup, evaluate your project by using the SWOT method: Identify the Strength, Weakness, Opportunity and Threat. Read Numbers 14. How can you avoid the pitfalls described in Numbers 14?

———————————————————————

———————————————————————

———————————————————————

———————————————————————

10. Imagine what the Kingdom of God would look like in your neighborhoods. What is your part in bringing it about? List 7 things that you can immediately start to work on toward your own and your community's transformation.

———————————————————————

———————————————————————

———————————————————————

———————————————————————

———————————————————————

### Annie Gonzales, *Cover Designer*

As a professional freelance graphic designer and art director of FHL International, I consult with my clients to create designs that express the passion of their project and let the glory of God shine through. Designing book covers, DVD and CD jackets, and all promotional materials, I prepare and provide your art for print and for your files. You may contact me at annie@fhlinternational.org and visit my online portfolio at fhlinternational.org.

### Janet Schwind, *Editor*

I partner with authors, editing and shaping manuscripts as well as providing project management and consulting to usher book projects efficiently through the self-publishing process. As liaison with the designer, I thoughtfully take your book from raw manuscript through editing, interior layout and cover design to print-ready. You can see my online portfolio at janetschwind.com or contact me at janetschwind@gmail.com.

### Suzanne Parada, *Book Designer*

As a professional independent book designer, I am committed to helping self-published authors produce their best book possible. I offer professional cover design and unique interior book layout providing files ready to be published via print-on-demand (POD) or traditional offset press. You can view samples on my website at paradadesign.com or contact me at s_parada@sbcglobal.net.

Merlin Gonzales was born in the Philippines. In 1984, he worked for a cruise line in Miami, FL, traveling through Europe and the Caribbean. In 1985, he moved to Indianapolis, IN where he later started his own business, leading him to relocate to several states. Experiencing the various cultures of these places opened his eyes to the core need of the human heart.

In 2003, with a desire to know the Word of God, he took a two-year study in church leadership and founded ConsumingFire Ministries. He was an Outreach Pastor from 2005 to 2009 where he implemented several evangelistic, discipleship and outreach programs. He has ministered to pastors and leaders in Indiana, Central and South America.

In 2005, Merlin founded Faith Hope and Love Intl., collaborating with churches, crossing denominational lines. With a passion to bring the love of Jesus into the community and through God's inspiration to unify the Body of Christ, Merlin has developed the concept of *Mission Trips in Your Own Backyard*, a week of backyard missions.

Merlin's teachings are about raising up a generation to live out the Kingdom culture - proclaiming, expressing and demonstrating the love of God, building a legacy of transformation. He is a Church Consultant helping pastors to reach out to their communities and to raise and train leaders.

Merlin lives in Noblesville, IN with his wife Annie and enjoys spending his free time with his two children, Kayla and Andrew.

# STATE OF INDIANA
## EXECUTIVE DEPARTMENT
### INDIANAPOLIS

Executive Order

# PROCLAMATION

### TO ALL TO WHOM THESE PRESENTS MAY COME, GREETINGS:

WHEREAS,     Faith, Hope, and Love is an annual week-long period of helping neighbors in our communities; and

WHEREAS,     The vision is to build communities of faith, hope and love through active participation in improving neighborhoods and by helping those in need; and

WHEREAS,     Faith, Hope, and Love Week brings together many churches, government entities, businesses and other organizations in the State of Indiana; and

WHEREAS,     Faith, Hope, and Love is about people participating in a joint effort to bridge the social, economic and spiritual gaps in our community;

NOW, THEREFORE, I, Mitchell E. Daniels, Jr., Governor of the State of Indiana, do hereby proclaim July 25-30, 2010 as

### Faith, Hope, and Love Week

in the State of Indiana, and invite all citizens to duly note this occasion.

*In Testimony Whereof, I hereto set my hand and cause to be affixed the Great Seal of State. Done at the City of Indianapolis, this 23rd day of March in the year of our Lord 2010 and of the Independence of the United States 233.*

BY THE GOVERNOR: _M E Daniels Jr._

Made in the USA
Charleston, SC
06 January 2013